DEALING CREATIVELY WITH DEATH

A Manual of Death Education
and Simple Burial

by Ernest Morgan

Celo Press
1901 Hannah Branch Road
Burnsville, NC 28714

Permission to Reprint: We are happy to be quoted, both to spread important ideas and to increase our circulation. Persons wishing to reprint a paragraph or two of material which is original to this book may do so if credit is given. Longer reprints by non-profit groups, not to exceed five pages, are welcomed if the following credit line is used: "from *Dealing Creatively with Death: A Manual of Death Education and Simple Burial*, by Ernest Morgan and published by Celo Press, Burnsville, NC 28714." We would appreciate it if you send us a copy of the publication you use our material in, or at least notify us of its use. For any other use of our material, please contact Celo Press Permissions Dept.

Library of Congress Cataloging in Publication Data

Morgan, Ernest.
 Dealing creatively with death.

 Rev. ed. of: A manual of death education & simple burial. 6th ed. 1973.
 Bibliography; p.
 includes index.
 1. Death. 2. Funeral rites and ceremonies— United States—Handbooks, manuals, etc. I. Morgan, Ernest. Manual of death education & simple burial. II. Title.
 BD444.M66 1984   363.7'5   83-71373
 ISBN 0-914064-19-3

Poems 40 (page 142), 46 and 49 (page 136) are reprinted with permission of Macmillan Publishing Company from *Fruit-Gathering*, by Rabindranath Tagore. Copyright © 1916 by Macmillan Publishing Co., Inc., renewed 1944 by Rathindranath Tagore.

Poems 84, 87 and 90 (page 135) are reprinted with permission of Macmillan Publishing Company from *Gitanjali*, by Rabindranath Tagore, copyright © 1916 by Macmillan Publishing Company.

ISBN 0-914064-19-3   LC No. 83-071373

TABLE OF CONTENTS

Why death education?; The growth of death education; About the death educator; Death education for
children; The greatest challenge; Other man-made
death; How to go about death education; Application
of the remaining chapters; References

A personal experience in home care; Supportive family and friends; My daughter's comments; The hospice movement; Models of hospice; An example of
hospice care; The future of hospice; The dying child;
Some general comments on dying; References

My own experience with grief; Group support in be-
reavement; Children and grief; The death of a child;
Suicide survivors; When someone causes a death;
Phases of grief; Support groups and professional help;
Avoid the use of drugs; How death illuminates life;
Catastrophic loss; Life after death; References

The right to refuse treatment; The deformed infant;
The problem of suicide; On communicating with potential suicides; Ground rules for self-termination;
Helping someone to die; "Respectable" forms of suicide; References

Why are most funerals so costly?; Regulation of the
funeral industry; Where to go with complaints; What
are the options for body disposition?; What's the difference between funeral and memorial services?; The
practice of simplicity; The need for planning; Thou-

eye banks in the U.S. and Canada); The bequeathal of bodies to schools of medicine and dentistry (why they are needed, procedure at time of death, a deeply meaningful experience, transportation of the remains, alternative plans); Directory of medical schools in the U.S. and Canada with key to their degree of need and the amount, if any, paid for body transportaion; Specific anatomical gifts (ear drums and ear bones, kidneys, livers, hearts, pancreas, lungs, pituitary glands, skin, blood, brain tissue, other tissues, artificial implants); References

Suggestions Welcomed

This book has been growing for 24 years and through ten editions. Much of the material in it has been referred to us by our readers.

We are continuing this practice and invite our readers to send us criticisms and information which may be useful in future editions.

About Celo Press and the Arthur Morgan School

As you may already know, Celo Press is the Printing and Publishing Department of the Arthur Morgan School, and proceeds from the book are used to help support the school.

The Arthur Morgan School is a small, innovative boarding and day school for boys and girls in the 7th, 8th and 9th grades. It is a living/learning community where, in addition to the academic program, the work and decision-making of daily life are shared by students and staff. Information about the school will be sent on request.

The school and Celo Press are on the land of Celo Community, an "intentional community"—the oldest land trust community in America—located in a beautiful mountain valley between the Black Mountains and the Blue Ridge.

Amongst the multitude of people who have helped me over the years with various writing projects, I count Ernest Morgan as *primus inter pares*—first among equals.

In the early 1960's, when I was preparing *The American Way of Death*, I ran across his *Manual of Simple Burial*—a brilliant little volume of advice to the hapless survivor who wants to avoid the full-fig funeral, with all the costly trimmings, decreed by the undertakers as what they are pleased to call "the standard American funeral."

Once, years ago, Ernest Morgan and I shared a flight from Seattle to Oakland. In the course of our conversation I asked what motivated him to continue active in the field of Death Education and Simple Burial. He looked out the window for a while, then he said, "There are three reasons. First, working in this field is contributing to my own emotional maturity—my acceptance of death, my appreciation of life and my concern for my fellow beings.

"Second, I'm devoted to social change, looking toward a more humane and cooperative society. At no other time are people more prone to think about their life values, and more open to change, than they are at a time of death, or in thinking about death. This is a strategic time to influence them in a creative way, and to overcome what is phony, exploitative and ostentatious in American life.

"Third, the *Manual* is making money for the Arthur Morgan School!"

Mr. Morgan and I became firm penpals and have corresponded for two decades. He was immeasurably helpful in giving guidance and practical advice when I was writing *The American Way of Death*, and for years thereafter as we fought in our respective communities what one writer called "the battle of the Bier Barons."

Unlike the *Manual*, my own book does not purport to deal with philosophic approaches to death and dying; it is merely an account of the funeral industry. In his review of *The American Way of Death*, Evelyn Waugh wrote that "the trouble with Miss Mitford is that she has no stated attitude towards death." I wrote to my sister

Nancy, who was a great friend of Waugh's, "Please tell Evelyn that I *do* have an attitude towards death. I'm against it." (When I told Ernest Morgan this, he commented in his wry, dry fashion, "Better not abolish death. If we do, people will need a government permit to have a baby!")

In contrast with earlier editions of the *Manual*, this expanded version, while retaining its useful information about memorial societies, bequeathal of remains to medical schools, etc. goes more deeply into the practical and philosophical concerns of death and dying.

His perceptive, humane views on these matters should provide great solace to the terminally ill and their families.

— *Jessica Mitford*

My father, Arthur E. Morgan, was an intensely creative man whose activities had a lasting impact in several areas of American life. He had long felt that American funeral practices could be simpler and more meaningful. Finally, in 1948, he formed the Burial Committee of the Yellow Springs Friends Meeting (Quaker) to study the matter in a systematic way.

After five years of study and correspondence this committee evolved a plan whereby the Meeting would care for its own dead, handling the paper work, building the boxes, conveying the bodies to a crematory and arranging memorial services—all without professional assistance.

In 1953 I was drafted by the Meeting to chair this committee. I had no special interest in the project but did not wish to avoid responsibility, so I accepted. After all, I thought, I am a grown man, I can probably handle a dead body as well as the next fellow.

During that five years of study no one in the Meeting had died, but as soon as I became chairman they started dying! Then I discovered that what I had anticipated to be a disagreeable chore turned out to be a meaningful privilege—serving one's friends at a time of profound need. The plan worked well at small cost, and the memorial services became a comfort and an inspiration to all concerned.

Then an incident occurred which brought a fresh dimension into my activities. The Dayton (Ohio) Unitarian Church called a meeting to organize a memorial society. Those people were friends of mine, so I came to the meeting and spoke of how the Yellow Springs Quakers handled their arrangements. Among those present at the meeting was Mildred Jensen Loomis, editor/publisher of *The Interpreter* (now *The Green Revolution*). She then wrote an article on my remarks for her newspaper.

The first thing I knew letters began pouring in. Gosh, I thought, I can't answer all these letters, I'll mimeograph a few sheets to send these people. Then another thought occurred to me. A burial committee is fine for a close-knit rural group like ours, but in most situations a memorial society which works with funeral directors is more practical. I'd better include some information on memorial societies. So I started digging out this information. (There was no memorial society association then.)

Then another thing happened. My stepmother, Lucy Morgan, asked me to go to Columbus and make arrangements for her to leave her body to the University Medical School. She was a thrifty soul. "I don't want my body wasted," she said. So I went and met Dr.

Graves (!) who was dean of the Anatomy department. Dr. Graves was (almost too) enthusiastic. "If only more people would do this! There's a serious shortage of bodies in many areas." So I saw that I'd better tell people about leaving their bodies to a medical school.

To make a long story short, another five years passed and, instead of a few mimeographed sheets I had a 64-page book, *A Manual of Simple Burial.* It first appeared in the fall of 1962, printed by Celo Press, a division of the Arthur Morgan School which my wife and I were launching then. The book was well received.

In 1963 another unexpected event occurred. The Co-op League of the U.S.A. called an international meeting to federate the memorial societies of the U.S. and Canada. Would I be a keynote speaker? I seemed to have become some kind of an authority. So I went and the next thing I knew I was on the Board of the Continental Association of Funeral and Memorial Societies. Who was it said, "There is a destiny that shapes our ends..."?

The book sold well and brought revenue to the school. New editions followed, each one extensively revised. Howard Raether, Executive Secretary of the National Funeral Directors Association once asked me, "How come you change the book so much between editions?" All I could say was, "Times keep changing, and new ideas and information keep coming."

One of the things that I learned was that most people turned their backs on the reality of death and were thus inhibited from joining a memorial society or planning ahead. Thus, death education was a prerequisite for coming to grips with the question. So, with our sixth edition we changed the title to *A Manual of Death Education and Simple Burial.* Sales continued to grow.

In 1971 my wife died of cancer after a long illness. During her final months we kept her at home where her life could be filled with love and fellowship and music. This was my introduction to what we now call hospice. Another dimension was thus added to the *Manual.*

Looking back, I realize that much of the book has been derived from the experience of a long life in a warm, cohesive family where death was a repeated visitor, and from half a century in a small community where life and death were deeply shared. That was my university, which has been supplemented and enhanced by reading and by association with many knowledgeable people.

No one has benefited more from reading this book than I have from writing it. As a child I was devoted to my father, a man of great strength and gentleness. Accepting his death was hard for me and writing this *Manual* made it possible for me to face reality and accept his death and that of others whom I have loved.

The *Manual* is no longer "my" book, but belongs as well to a host of friends and scholars who have helped with it. In particular, my daughter Jenifer has done much of the research and writing for this edition and has been my most faithful and exacting critic. Now in my 79th year (1984) I hope that she will have an even greater hand in future editions, and will carry it on when I'm gone.

— *Ernest Morgan*

If we were to walk across the fields in summertime to some undisturbed spot and mark off a piece of ground say four feet square and then examine this little area minutely, we would find an astonishing variety of life. There would be many species of plants—possibly a mouse's nest and certainly a considerable variety of insects, spiders, centipedes and other small creatures. Then, resorting to a microscope, we would observe an incredible host of microorganisms functioning in association with the larger life forms. But we would not stop there. We would start digging, exploring for additional life underground. There, too, we would find insects, nematodes, earthworms of various kinds, and a fresh array of bacteria. Nor would we necessarily stop when we reached bedrock. If that rock happened to be Ohio limestone there would be several hundred feet of dense fossil deposits laid down through millions of years, representing myriad species and astronomical numbers of individual lives.

In that little square of ground we would have seen an interdependent community of life in which birth and death were continuously taking place and in which diverse life forms were sheltering and nourishing one another. Written in the rocks beneath was a story of a similar process going back through eons of time.

Mankind is part of the ongoing community of nature, on a world scale, subject to the same cycle of birth and death which governs all other creatures and, like them, totally dependent on other life. Sometimes, in our high-rise apartments, our manicured suburbs and our chromium plated institutions we tend to forget this.

Our need is not to conquer nature but to live in harmony with it. This does not mean rejecting our technology, but it does mean controlling our numbers, quieting our egos, and simplifying lifestyles.

Birth and death are as natural for us as for the myriad creatures in that little square of ground. When we have learned to accept ourselves as part of the community of nature, then we can accept death as part of the natural order of things.

We commonly act as if we, and those we love, were going to live forever. But we are wrong, for all must die—nor can we know when this will happen.

In our culture we tend to avoid the subject of death. This is unfortunate, for death is a normal and necessary part of life. Until we learn to face it honestly and accept it, we are not living at our best.

If we are to appreciate our fellows, if we are to live with patience, gentleness and love, let us be about it today, for life is short.

Ernest Morgan

I / DEATH EDUCATION

This chapter has three functions.

First is to break the ice—for those who need to have it broken—and help people feel at ease in talking about death. Until they are able to do this without feeling uncomfortable they will have difficulty in benefiting from the ensuing chapters.

Second is to review briefly the emergence of death education and to discuss some of the ways in which it is strongly relevant to life, both of the individual and of society.

Third, this chapter gives a brief overview of the rest of the book, suggesting possible uses of the remaining chapters, and offering suggestions for persons who may be leading classes or discussions on the topic.

In the preparation of this chapter we received extensive help from Ed Knapp, of the Forum for Death Education and Counseling, and from Tom Plaut, of Mars Hill College, both of whom assisted also with the chapter on Bereavement.

— Ernest and Jenifer

Why Death Education?

Death education is for everyone, because it relates not just to death but to our feelings about ourselves and nature and the universe we live in. A prime function of death education is to help us to think and feel deeply about the meaning of life in its many relationships—to help mature our values. As Abraham Maslow wrote, after recovering from a heart attack, "The confrontation with death—and the reprieve from it—makes everything look so precious, so sacred, so beautiful that I feel more strongly than ever the impulse to love it, to embrace it and to let myself be overwhelmed by it."[1] Confronting death imaginatively through experience, reading, thinking, lectures and discussions often has the paradoxical effect of enriching life.

As we pass beyond the fear and avoidance of death so common in our culture, we can learn to accept dying as an appropriate culmination of life. To do this we need to be able to talk freely with our loved ones about death—both our own and theirs, whether imminent or remote.

Death education does not avoid grief—and should not if it could—but it can help us to cope with grief in a creative way so that we may grow in the quality of our lives. It can help us also to relate meaningfully to dying persons, and to meet the social and emotional needs of the survivors—including ourselves.

Then, too, it can help us deal wisely with practical matters that must be faced at time of death, thus avoiding unnecessary ostentation, suffering and expense.

Death education is doubly valuable for those whose work brings them into frequent contact with dying, death and/or bereavement. These include not only health professionals, counselors and clergy, but also law enforcement, military and disaster personnel who work with survivors of major loss and sudden death.

The Growth of Death Education

Twenty-five years ago the subject of death was taboo in polite society, as sex had been in earlier days. In 1959, Dr. LeRoy Bowman's sociological study, *The American Funeral*, and Herman Feifel's *The Meaning of Death* cracked the barrier. In 1962 the first edition of my *Manual* appeared, followed in 1963 by Ruth Harmer's *The High Cost of Dying* and Jessica Mitford's bombshell, *The American Way of Death*. That same year the memorial societies emerged, largely under church leadership, as a united, continent-wide movement.

In 1967 Earl Grollman's *Explaining Death to Children* was published, and in 1969 Elisabeth Kubler-Ross gave the movement fresh depth and impetus with her classic *On Death and Dying*, stressing the need for death education among health care professionals. Since that time, hundreds of books and thousands of articles have appeared.

In 1975 the Forum for Death Education and Counseling was organized, giving form and substance to the movement, and in 1983 reported over 1,000 members working professionally in the field. Thousands of schools and colleges now have classes in death education. Many churches likewise conduct seminars and conferences on the subject. Important, too, it has become a significant topic in courses in social and psychological subjects and the health care disciplines as well as in literature, law, art, biology, philosophy and religion and consumer education.

Simultaneously, hospice programs began in the U.S. The National Hospice Organization was formed in 1977 to provide national leadership in education, research, standard setting and advocacy. Hospices now train thousands of volunteers and professionals to deal humanely with dying and death. (See Chapter II.)

Clearly, death education is coming into its own.

About the Death Educator

The educator and counselor needs to deepen his/her own understanding and acceptance of death and dying. It is this understanding, combined with personal experience, which qualifies one to teach. It is the ability to share this experience and understanding directly from the heart that makes a fine teacher.

Similarly, an important qualification—perhaps the most important qualification—for anyone to counsel bereaved persons is that the counselor has dealt creatively with suffering and is able to reach out to, and empathize with, the person being counseled. Most such counselors—at least the good ones—have been drawn into the field by virtue of their own experience and what they have learned from it.

Such counseling, at its best, is a two-way experience in which the counselor as well as the counseled experiences growth. That is one of the rewards of being a counselor.

Death Education for Children

Children have more awareness of death than most of us realize. Fairy tales, movies and television programs abound in death, as does the world of nature which they see about them.

Herman Feifel comments that "The shaping impact of awareness of death is active at all levels."[2] By age two, children's play demonstrates an awareness of death. Children three to five years of age commonly see death as temporary and reversible. From about five to nine years of age the finality is recognized and children begin to understand that death is an inevitable part of life. At first they think of it as something that happens to others but not to themselves; later they realize it will someday happen to them. By age ten, if not before, most children understand the reality of death as adults do.[3]

Acceptance of death as part of life needs to be incorporated into a child's normal activities at home and at school. On the occasion of deaths in my own family, the children were kept close to the center of family life and given roles to carry out in family activities relating to the deaths. This gave comfort to the adults as well as to the children.

While wildly emotional outbursts may be upsetting to children, adults should not try to conceal their emotions from their children. Naturalness and honesty are basic. The physical fact of death should be explained and children should not be discouraged from touching dead things if they wish. It should be explained that dead things feel no pain, as children commonly have great fear of pain. It helps to explain that we are part of the world of nature and share with all other creatures the cycle of life and death. For each of us there is a time to be born, to grow and flourish, and then to die. Fears are lessened if the emphasis is on the beauty of life.

The Greatest Challenge

Perhaps death education's greatest challenge—and maybe its greatest potential for usefulness, too—is in the issue of man-made death.

The fear of death—especially massive, man-made death—can lead to despair and increased self-destructiveness. Why prepare for a career or cultivate serious interests and skills, when the entire future is in doubt? Why not take indiscriminate refuge in alcohol, drugs and sex? Edgar Jackson suggests that young people today are engaging in "giant funerals," acting out their deep concern for the world's future.[4]

Even more dangerous is the way in which people respond to their fear of death by threatening death to others. As Dr. Kubler-Ross has said, "Groups of people, from street gangs to nations, may express their fear of being destroyed by attacking and destroying others. Is war, perhaps ... a need to face death, to conquer and master it, to come out of it alive—a peculiar form of denial of our own mortality?"[5]

This urge to conquer death is often associated with some of the noblest human sentiments: courage, loyalty and unselfishness, along with strong identification with one's social group—ethnic, national, religious or other, and the normal feeling that one's life will be carried on through that group.

Danger lies in the need to believe in the absolute rightness of one's nation or cause—and the absolute evil of some enemy. Then one's own acts, however aggressive they may be, can be seen as justified defense or retaliation. In addition, one carries the "survivor mission" of perpetuating past victories, avenging old defeats, repaying a "debt of honor" to those who have given their lives, as expressed in John McCrae's poem, popular during World War I:

> Take up the quarrel with the foe;
> To you from failing hands we throw
> The torch; be yours to hold it high.
> If ye break faith with us who die,
> We shall not sleep, though poppies grow
> In Flanders fields.[6]

Seeking transcendence over death by such national and ethnic loyalty can, in this nuclear age, lead to catastrophic results. Death education can help us to understand and change this pattern.

Similarly, death education can help us cope with the tendency to despair. Commenting on the nuclear menace, sociologist Henrik Infield exclaimed, "If we're going to be blown up, let's be blown up doing something worthwhile!" In other words, we should accept the reality of the dangers that face us, then place our bets on life!

There are constructive ways in which we can deal with the prospect of human extinction. To take a hand in our own destiny, even on a tiny scale, improves our chances and, besides, gives us a sense of empowerment which is essential to our emotional well-being.

A teacher in Seattle asked her students: "How many of you think there might be a nuclear war?" Hands were raised by every child but one. "And you, Sally, why aren't you expecting that?"

"Well, Mommy and Daddy are working for disarmament and I think they're going to win."

Human solidarity is important. For an old-timer like myself, there is a temptation to take refuge in the thought that I'm likely to be dead and gone before hell breaks loose. But I quickly reject this impulse as cowardice and take my stand with the young people who will inherit the future. We can't avoid our individual deaths, but we can try, by thoughtful and concerted action, to avoid the death of our civilization. This idea can give us inspiration and hope.

Other Man-Made Death

War is not the only form of man-made death that needs to be dealt with openly. There are other difficult social questions, such as capital punishment, abortion, euthanasia, accidental deaths and suicide. Some of these issues are beyond the scope of this book, but euthanasia and suicide are dealt with at length in Chapter IV, "The Right to Die."

How to Go About Death Education

First of all, consider the makeup and needs of the class. Is it a high school or college group? Is it made up of hospice volunteers who need to relate to dying persons? Is it a group of health professionals and, if so, at what level? Is it an adult seminar including people with problems of grief and loss? Is it for church people considering plans for their own last rites and arrangements, or perhaps planning a support group for assisting bereaved families?

This has a bearing on the topics to be included and what emphasis to give to each. Lecture and discussion topics, films, books and field trips may be selected from a wide range of possibilities. It helps to prepare a detailed syllabus so that the class will know what to expect.

The teacher needs to be sensitive to the particular needs s/he is dealing with and the feelings that may be evoked. It helps to circulate a questionnaire to the members of the class at the outset, including such questions as: "Why are you taking this course?", "What was your most significant experience with death?", "Do you have any special death-related experiences which you bring to the class?"

In all class discussions and role playing, participation should be voluntary and students should not be pressed for answers. Offering alternative assignments can allow students to decide whether or not to approach an emotionally difficult subject. Suggested questions for discussion, resource people, and role play ideas are provided in Appendix III.

Application of the Remaining Chapters

Each chapter of this Manual presents a topic or topics that may be included in a syllabus.

"Living with Dying," stressing home care for the terminally ill, will be of special interest to hospice workers and other health care personnel. Churches may use it to help in supporting home care for parishioners. Memorial Society members and others will be interested in planning to meet their families' needs. Family life courses should include this.

"Bereavement" is an essential topic for all of us, as experience of loss is universal. Hospice workers are committed to bereavement support; every counselor, clergyman and health care worker needs the information this chapter provides. Churches will find it helpful in encouraging congregational support of the bereaved in the church community. Students of drama, psychology and sociology will find it a resource.

"The Right to Die" is of special interest to persons facing terminal illness within their families and to those who wish to make provision in advance to assure that they will have some control over their own deaths. Likewise it is of interest to all persons involved in health care, including, of course, hospice workers. Students of law and philosophy also will find this frequently controversial presentation interesting. The last part of this chapter deals in depth with the increasingly urgent problem of suicide and the role of the teacher in dealing with this problem.

"Simple Burial and Cremation" presents the philosophy and practice of planning for and handling a death in the family in a simple manner—information every family should have. Professionals and volunteers who work with the dying can be of great service in making this information available. Church leaders, too, will want this information to meet the needs of their religious communities. As with memorial societies, this topic should be included in consumer education.

"Memorial Societies" should be understood by all who work with death and dying—or who expect to die someday! They have a unique role in assisting families who desire simplicity and economy in funeral arrangements.

"Death Ceremonies" are very important in meeting the social and emotional needs of survivors at a time of death. This chapter has been included at the request of several readers who felt the need for alternative types of ceremonies that would better meet these needs. This chapter is useful to church people and others who may be concerned with planning a service. Special attention is given to memorial services.

"How the Dead Can Help the Living" is to encourage people to make anatomical gifts at the time of death, and tells how to plan accordingly. This is an urgent concern at the present time, of special relevance to health professionals, biologists and lawyers.

Extensive material, including a selected bibliography on Death Education, has been assembled in the Appendix at the back of this book, where it will be updated with each new printing.

REFERENCES

[1] From a letter to Dr. Rollo May, as it appeared in *Love and Will*, by Rollo May. W.W. Norton, 1969. Used with permission.

[2] Herman Feifel, "The Meaning of Death in American Society," in *Death Education*, by Donald Irish and Betty Green (Cambridge, MA: Schenkman Publishing Company, 1971), p. 5.

[3] De Spelder & Strickland, *The Last Dance: Encountering Death & Dying* (Palo Alto, CA: Mayfield Publishing Co., 1983) includes a good summary of developmental studies of children's concepts of death.

[4] Donald Irish & Betty Green, *op. cit.*, p. 57.

[5] Elisabeth Kubler-Ross, *On Death and Dying* (New York: Macmillan Publishing Co., 1969), p. 11.

[6] *1000 Quotable Poems: An Anthology of Modern Verse*, compiled by Thomas Curtis Clark and Esther A. Gillespie (New York: Harper & Brothers, 1937). (Apparently this poem was first published in London, England, in *Punch*.)

II / LIVING WITH DYING

In this chapter I tell of my experience in caring for a dying patient at home and discuss how to relate to a dying person in a positive way. Also discussed are group support for the family of a dying person and how to relate to a dying child. These things are described as part of the Hospice concept, which has given rise to a strong movement in the past ten years. This also is discussed in some detail. Appendix IV reviews financial help available for home care. I am indebted to friends in the Hospice movement, especially Sally Burrowes of the Yancey County Hospice Organization, for help with this chapter.   *— Ernest*

A Personal Experience in Home Care

I had never heard of the hospice philosophy in 1971 when my wife, Elizabeth, was dying of cancer, but my daughter and I had the basic concept. It was Elizabeth's wish to spend her last weeks at home, so we brought her there.

This was a family decision, as an alternative to institutional care. Desirable as home care may be, it is not for everyone, nor is it appropriate in every situation. The preference of the patient should be respected. Some may prefer the security of institutional care. Equally important is the genuine desire and ability of the family to provide the needed care. Half of the older people in nursing homes have no significant family relationship.[1]

If you do decide on home care, you don't need a degree in nursing to do most of the things that are required. My daughter got instructions at the hospital and then passed them along to me—how to give shots, change bedding, give baths and take care of toilet needs. How to take pulse and temperature we already knew, and keeping a hospital chart was a simple routine. The chief requirement was willingness, and the desire to do it. It wasn't

nearly as difficult as we had expected and was made easier because we loved the patient.

We had a good working relationship with the doctor, who
knew that my wife and daughter and I were united in our desire for
home care and that we had realistic plans for providing it. We were
on the phone with him every couple of days, and he helped make
medical decisions and prescribe medicines. Had Medicare or other
insurance applied, the doctor's authorization would have met their
requirements.

Some doctors find it difficult to work with dying patients and
their families. Because of this it is important to talk to your doctor
about home care and be assured that s/he will be comfortable answering your questions and respect your views concerning care of
a dying person. Try to find a doctor you feel good about working
with.

·Equipment was not a serious problem. We borrowed a hospital bed, an overbed table and a commode chair, and contrived a
stand for the intravenous fluids from a sturdy music rack. Such
incidentals as a rubber sheet and bedpan were purchased or borrowed. Local home health or hospital nurses and social workers
can help locate sources of such things. At intervals a nurse from
the health department came and started the I.V., which we moni-
tored and stopped at the right time.

Elizabeth experienced chronic pain, which was controlled by
shots given as instructed by the doctor whenever she called for
them. Variations of the Brompton Cocktail, which was developed
by St. Christopher's Hospice in London, or other narcotics given
orally, now usually eliminate the need for frequent injections.
When medication is given on a regular schedule the patient does
not have to call for relief or wait in anticipation of pain. Eliminating
the fear and stress associated with chronic pain often lessens the
pain itself. With careful and continuing adjustment of dosages,
good alertness usually can be retained while pain is controlled.

Supportive Family and Friends

It was in the area of non-technical resources, however, that home
care excelled. My wife was surrounded by loving family members
and friends. She loved music and was a fine musician, so by her bed
we put an FM radio that brought in several National Public Radio
stations. (Bless NPR!) She tried to have a visit with each of her students before she died, and family and friends from far and near

came to see her. Some sang for her—folk songs and gospel hymns. Often they embraced her. It was a warmly human situation.

Elizabeth's acceptance of death was helped, not only by her family's acceptance of it, but by turning much of her attention and emotional energies outside herself. As her strength permitted, she talked with the young people she knew, discussing their problems and plans. I recall an evening at the hospital, before she came home. Talking with the doctor, she said, "There's a little girl at school to whom I've promised the lead in next year's operetta, and she needs it so badly! I've just got to have another year." The doctor had tears in his eyes when he left the room, and he put her back on chemotherapy for one more try.

Elizabeth was able to read a fair amount and delved into philosophy and science, maturing her own philosophy, which we wrote down for her. I read aloud her favorite poetry, including some beautiful pieces on death.

Often a dying person seeks perspective on the meaning of his or her life, a sense of what has been accomplished. What seems to be garrulousness in an old person may be part of this "life review." Other people can help by allowing time for listening, reflection, sharing family pictures, perhaps taking down memoirs by hand or tape.[2]

Elizabeth accepted the prospect of death calmly, almost cheerfully, but fought hard for life. We prepared "green drinks" and other things said sometimes to cause remissions, and none of us gave up hope until the very end. Even when death is accepted and seems certain, an element of hope is meaningful.

We knew she was going to die, and we talked about it frankly. This was very important. Dying persons should be allowed to accept the reality of their situation at their own pace. Information should neither be withheld from them nor thrust upon them. Ordinarily they will ask for it.

Becoming aware of one's own dying enables a person to complete "unfinished business"—to say goodbye, perhaps to mend damaged relationships, or to tend to disposition of possessions and make final arrangements. To practice deceit toward a dying person can be poisonous, both to the patient and to the family, which may later bitterly regret having missed the chance for open communication of feelings. Such deception also limits the "anticipatory grieving" that a family can do and thus intensifies the shock and grief when the death occurs. Elizabeth told me shortly before she died how much it meant to her that we were able to accept her death. Some dying persons whose families would not accept their death or talk about it have written me, a stranger, to fill this void.

There was at that time no hospice organization, but we had strong community support. Friends ran errands and did shopping for us and gave a hand wherever needed. Similarly, Josefina Magno, first Executive Director of the National Hospice Organization, tells of a woman whose wish to die at home was realized because her synagogue organized help to assist with her care.

My wife was afraid that her death might upset the students at the Arthur Morgan School, with whom she had a very close relationship. Accordingly I prepared a talk, telling of her condition and discussing life and death. We worked this over to our satisfaction and then I gave it to the students. They received it thoughtfully and seemed to benefit from it.

One of these students, a few years later, himself died of bone cancer following the amputation of both legs. He maintained a buoyant spirit throughout and was very supportive of his parents in their distsress. The family psychological counselor told me afterwards that the fine spirit shown by this boy directly reflected his experience of Elizabeth Morgan's death.

Clearly, my daughter and I and the friends who supported us were required to make an emotional investment in my wife's care. This is the case in any good hospice situation, for family, volunteers and professionals alike. But this investment brings valuable returns—in maturity and strength, in deepened values, in relief of guilt, in drawing the family closer together and in an altered awareness of self in relation to social reality.

As Elisabeth Kubler-Ross says, "Those who have the strength and the love to sit with a dying patient in the silence that goes beyond words will know that this moment is neither frightening nor painful. ... Watching a peaceful death is like watching a falling star."[3] Elizabeth's actual death was peaceful, as she quietly stopped breathing.

My Daughter's Comments

When we knew that Mother was losing her two-year battle with cancer, I was glad to be in a position to bring my two children, then ten and twelve years old, and help take care of her. My sister-in-law stayed with her and Dad the first month she was home from the hospital, and then I came. Dad bought an old house trailer and set it up nearby for us to stay in. I went to the hospital and learned about giving shots, caring for a colostomy and general practical nursing.

Because there were two of us, we could take turns caring for Mother, and I had time to be with the children and go out occasionally with friends. We shared the general housework and physical care of Mother, while I did most of the cooking and each evening gave her a backrub, which seemed to be especially comforting.

Luckily I had a support group in the form of a peer counseling group with which I met weekly. (Mostly we took turns listening to each other.) Through this, one friend learned of the struggle I was having caring for one of my children, whose personality clashed with Mother's, and she invited my child to stay with her family for awhile. That helped a lot, though oftentimes I still felt torn in the evenings between spending evening time with the children and doing the evening routines that would ease Mother's nights. Through all this I learned how important it is to consider the needs of children in the family when planning home care for the dying. Sometimes this alone is sufficient reason not to attempt home care.

Cooking presented its own problems. Mother's tastes and needs were simple—she especially loved lamb chops and baked custard—but one effect of the cancer was to upset the digestive system so that nothing really tasted good or digested easily. It was near the end of her illness that I became aware of the painful sense of inadequacy that this caused me. Certainly helplessness to meet the needs of a loved one who is suffering is in itself a major stress.

The control of pain presented some difficulties, too. The medicines we used tended to make Mother groggy, so she tried to use as little as possible, torn between full but painful consciousness and partial abandonment of her selfhood. The constant use of shots in itself became increasingly painful. I'm glad that pain control is better now. Studies still show, however, that there is much unnecessary pain caused by restraints of law and custom on drugs considered addictive.[4]

In spite of these problems, Mother had a remarkably buoyant and outgoing spirit, responding with vibrant enthusiasm to the people, music and ideas that she loved. It was a great gift to me to learn so much about the transcendence of pain and acceptance of death.

The Hospice Movement

Hospice is a declaration of the dignity and humanness of people who have not long to live, and the determination that their last months and weeks and days shall be lived fully with as much fellowship, affection and comfort as possible. More specifically, hospice is a specialized health care program for the terminally ill, making the family the unit of care through both the dying and the period of bereavement.

In the preceding paragraphs I told something of my own experiences with death and the ways in which I was helped by friends and professionals alike. These experiences took place before the rise of the hospice movement and I was fortunate to get the help I did.

The situation is rapidly improving, with over 600 hospice programs now organized. You can find out if there is one in your area by contacting your county health department or home health service, a hospital social worker or chaplain, the National Hospice Organization, or one of the state organizations listed in Appendix IV.

Most hospice programs provide for a multi-disciplinary team to work with the family, including a doctor who provides medical supervision, a nurse who monitors day-to-day care and coordinates the team, a counselor (usually social worker or pastor), volunteers to assist and relieve the family and others as needed. The goal is that all who serve the family will work together, learning from each other and providing a unified approach to care and treatment. Most hospices provide twenty-four-hour, seven-day-a-week accessibility of services, since crises may arise at any time. For a patient to be eligible for the services of most hospices, death must be anticipated within a limited time, usually six to twelve months.

Models of Hospice Care

Historically, hospice meant a place, an actual building—a refuge. This is the meaning at the forty-four-bed St. Christopher's Hospice in London, founded in 1967, which has been a model and inspiration for the hospice movement in North America. In addition to a few freestanding hospices in the U.S., some hospitals and nursing homes now have special units for hospice, or palliative care, sometimes in a separate building, or adapting treatment of dying patients through use of volunteers, special training for staff, more homelike environments, and counseling for the patient and family.

In the United States, a majority of hospice programs operate as home care programs, with no in-patient facility. Often a person who is being cared for at home will spend brief periods in a hospital or nursing home for treatment of acute symptoms or respite for the family. Most hospital or freestanding facilities, on the other hand, encourage the patient to spend as much time at home as possible.

With the cost of health care estimated to be doubling every 7½ years, some 40% of people can expect their last illness to cost more than all their previous health care combined. Hospice-assisted home care can ease this problem. The hospice in our rural mountain county recently estimated they had saved $500,000 in hospital bills for their patients in 18 months.

An Example of Hospice Care

The following piece, given to us by Sally Burrowes, or our local (Yancey County, N.C.) hospice organization, describes a recent experience. It indicates how the hospice spirit can and should find expression.

"I remember the first time you came up this hill, Jackie,"

"So do I, Claude. It must be just about four months ago."

"It's two months to the day since my Elsie died. I go up to the grave every day." The old man shook his head slowly. "I don't know how I'm going to make it. It's just so awful lonely."

The young woman put her hand over Claude's and held it gently. They were sitting at the top of the steep front steps, looking out over the valley to the blue mountains beyond. A pale March sun, promising daffodils, had drawn them out of the house for their visit.

"It's been a long winter, hasn't it, Claude?"

"Why, yes." He reached for his handkerchief and straightened his shoulders. "It has been that. ... And a long road since we brought Elsie home like she wanted and you first came and then the others."

Jackie smiled. "I remember seeing Elsie tucked up in your big old bed and you trying to put clean sheets on it with her not able to turn over and the bed smack up against the wall in the corner. Elsie liked to joke about that, didn't she?"

"Oh, Elsie was a strong woman and right cheerful all the time—always. I'm good for nothin' without her." Claude paused, then stood up. "There's all those bills from doctors and from that time way back in the hospital that still keep coming. I know I paid my part of that one bill, but they keep sayin' I've not.''

"Let me have the last bill you got, Claude. I'll see what I can find out about it."

"I never should of put her in the hospital at all. Then she'd never of gotten so sick as to die. I feel real bad over that. It seems like my fault."

"It always seemed to me that you did the very best you could, Claude. You were a real steady, loving caregiver for Elsie."

"Well—"

They went into the small tidy house. Where the hospital bed had stood all those weeks there was an empty space. Jackie looked out the window which framed Elsie's last pleasures in snow on the garden patch, a redbird in the old pear tree, the coming of one child and another to visit, to help, and, finally, to vigil. The two sons and a daughter lived not too far but they all worked full time. Jackie picked up a photograph from the dresser.

"You have some very handsome grandchildren, Claude. Remember how young Bill used to come every day after school to be with you and his grandma? And the day he brought Elsie the beautiful orange cat from the school fair and you decided you better learn to like cats after all? And next to him is Linda, who spent the night so many times in hopes you'd get some rest."

"They still come by pretty often. It helps against some of the lonesomeness."

Jackie replaced the pictures. They moved on into the bright spotless kitchen. "Linda will make a good nurse when she graduates," Jackie said.

"Well, Linda sure admired the one who was our Hospice nurse, that nurse McLain. She had a calm and gentle way with Elsie—and with me. She'd write out when to give the pills and tell us how to keep Elsie from bed sores and how to use the aspirator for her comfort and not to be surprised if Elsie went through a time of confusion and agitation before the end. She'd keep in touch with the doctor for the best pain medicine and be right there with us if things got real bad." Claude turned toward Jackie. "We could never of kept Elsie here at home without nurse McLain and all the rest of you."

"You know that's just what Hospice volunteers are for, Claude."

"Well. That Kate would bring fresh-laid eggs and sit with Elsie while I went for prescriptions or to market. She still comes by like you, ever so often, for a visit. Then there was George. Haven't seen much of him lately."

'George has a new job that's keeping him pretty busy."

"Well, he was a real help picking apples that day. And he helped get the hospital bed back to Hospice even before the funeral—so it didn't sit there all empty." Claude paused a moment. "You know," he said, "I was holding Elsie's hand at the very end. I think she was glad of that."

With a faint smile for a good thing remembered, he turned and reached for a cake in the corner cabinet.

"Charley's wife brought this yesterday. You have a piece now."

"Looks good, Claude. I'll have a piece if you do."

The old man cut two large slices. They sat at the shiny formica table and ate the cake under the winking stare of Elsie's orange cat and in the companionable silence of friendship grown through the shared caring for suffering and loss.

The Future of Hospice

The rapid growth of the hospice movement shows that it is an idea whose time has come. We can rejoice that people are asserting their need and right to a human and humane death and are acting to do something about it.

At the same time there is widespread concern that hospice may become commercialized, a package service that loses the caring qualities of sensitivity and individuality. Some of the experiences of exploitation and profiteering in the nursing home "industry" serve as a warning.

It is good that hospitals are coming to recognize and implement the hospice principle in appropriate cases. At the same time we agree with the National Hospice Organization that it is good to create and preserve autonomous hospice organizations as the main thrust of the movement. It would be unfortunate if the hospice movement as a whole were to find itself tied into the acute-care cost structure of modern hospitals.

Ideally hospice should exert a humanizing effect on all our health care institutions and activate a host of volunteers to assist with home care. It is interesting to note that at present hospice serves primarily cancer victims, who comprise only about twenty-five percent of those who die each year.[5] About half the deaths in the U.S. are from cardio-vascular ailments, and many people die in ambulances, emergency rooms and other settings where there is not time for hospice-type care. As we learn to accept and ease the process of dying, perhaps they, too, will benefit.

In the Appendix sections there are names and addresses of hospice organizations and books and publications relating to hospice.

The Dying Child[6]

"All children know," Dr. Kubler-Ross says, "(not consciously, but intuitively) about the outcome of their illness. All little ones are aware (not on an intellectual, but on a spiritual level) if they are close to death." They are also aware of the pain and worries of their families and cannot be fooled about them. She counsels parents: "Tell them you are sad and sometimes feel so useless that you cannot help more. They will hold you in their little arms and feel good that they can help you by sharing comfort. Shared sorrow is much easier to bear than leaving them with feelings of guilt and fear that they are the cause of all your anxiety."

While "false cheer" should be avoided, the family, and especially healthy children, should feel free to continue to laugh and play, bring friends home and lead a normal life as far as possible. "The worst thing we can do to the terminally ill child and the rest of the family is to make a morgue out of the house while the child is still living. Where there is laughter and joy, shared love, and little pleasures, the day-to-day difficulties are much easier to bear." Overprotection and over-indulgence are to be avoided as confusing both to the sick child and to other children who are not similarly treated.

Brothers and sisters should be informed and "become part of the care in one way or another." At home, they can do tasks appropriate to their ages and even in the hospital they can make cheerful decorations or play favorite music on a tape recorder. "Such illnesses are much harder on the brothers and sisters than they are on the patient," Dr. Kubler-Ross comments. By continuing a normal family life as far as possible, and being sure that family members or friends spend extra time with healthy brothers and sisters, these children can share in the experience of caring, love and grief without feelings of neglect or wishing the child would die so that normal family life can be resumed.

Support for families with children who are dying is as essential as in home care of an elderly person. Informal support structures or hospice organizations can offer strategic relief to the care-giving parent(s), and this is often overlooked.

Some General Comments on Dying

Dr. Kubler-Ross has enumerated some of the phases commonly experienced by dying people—denial and isolation, anger, bargaining, depression and acceptance. Kathy Charmaz[7] wisely adds that negative feelings on the part of the dying person often reflect, or are aggravated by, the rejection they experience on the part of those around them, especially in institutions. Where they continue to be warmly accepted as human beings by their family, friends, and care-givers, they can more easily accept their situation. In particular this is true where the persons about them are able to accept their death.

Sensitivity to the wishes of the dying person is central. Some like silence; others appreciate being spoken to. It has sometimes been found that persons who appear to be unconscious are, in fact, aware of what is being said. One woman, recovering from near death, remembered hearing a nurse say, "It's about time the old bitch died!" Quiet words of reminiscence and affection spoken to a seemingly unconscious dying person may, in fact, be giving final warmth and comfort to that person.

Often as death approaches a person feels less pain and wants less food. While ice chips are good to relieve dryness of the mouth, fluids swallowed may cause difficulties. A person near death often runs a high fever and feels hot, even while extremities are growing cold. The person may toss and turn trying to throw off coverings which are too warm. Like any immobilized person, one who is dying is more comfortable if turned on his or her side occasionally.

The dying person may begin to withdraw emotionally or lapse into unconsciousness. It is important to accept this withdrawal as a natural process, not as lack of love. Most, but not all, appreciate their hand being held. Nearly always the presence of a loved one is comforting.

He or she may be confused, or have hallucinations. This is sometimes considered to be part of a transition to a new existence as earthly ties are loosening. Breathing may be peaceful or intermittent with long pauses or may be labored and rasping. At death, as at birth, it is good to have someone there who has attended other deaths and knows what to expect.

Physical details to be attended to after death may include gently closing the eyes, closing the mouth and positioning the head on a pillow, and dressing the body if desired. This is easier in the first hour after death, before the body stiffens. Occasionally a body may empty the bladder or bowels reflexively after death.

An important advantage of death at home is that the family members who are there may sit with the body for a while. They may sit in silence, or talk to or about the patient, or pray. This time after death can be very helpful to survivors in beginning to adjust to the loss. This is an old practice in some cultures, and some hospitals will cooperate, especially if it is prearranged.

What is done next will depend on plans for the disposition of the body, and for memorial or funeral services. See Chapters V and VII, "Simple Burial and Cremation" and "Death Ceremonies."

It is my feeling that family members, especially children, who are at hand when someone dies or shortly after, should be encouraged to see the person who has died, but should not be urged. This may help them accept the reality of death. Cosmetic restoration, which makes the person appear lifelike, is no great help in this respect.

When my wife died, my daughter's two children were with me. I asked if they would care to see her before we put her body in the box. The girl said yes, the boy said no. That was all right on both counts. Again, there was no cosmetic work and no public viewing. The whole thing was low-keyed and natural.

REFERENCES

[1] Robert N. Butler, M.D., "The Need for Quality Hospice Care," address to National Hospice Organization, 1978, p. 8.

[2] Robert N. Butler, M.D., "Successful Aging and the Role of the Life Review," *Journal of the American Geriatrics Society*, 22:530 (1974).

[3] Elisabeth Kubler-Ross, *On Death and Dying* (New York: Macmillan Publishing Co., 1969), p. 246.

[4] M. Angell, "The Quality of Mercy," *New England Journal of Medicine*, 306:98-9 (1982). Documents failure to give adequate pain relief to terminal patients and examines reasons for this. Recommends change in law.

[5] Robert N. Butler, M.D., "The Need for Quality Hospice Care," *op. cit.*, p. 14.

[6] Quotations in this section are taken with permission from Elisabeth Kubler-Ross, *On Children and Death* (New York: Macmillan Publishing Co., 1983), pp. 1-3.

[7] Kathy Charmaz, *The Social Reality of Death* (Reading, MA: Addison-Wesley Publishing Company, 1980).

III / BEREAVEMENT

*Largely autobiographical, this chapter surveys the problems
of bereavement and grief and offers positive ways of coping with
these experiences so that they may contribute to personal growth.*
— Ernest

Grief is a normal reaction to the loss of a person, thing or relationship for which we have cared deeply. The only way to avoid grief is to die young before anyone you love has preceded you, or to never care for anyone—in a word, to reject life. Our problem is not to avoid grief but to deal with it wisely and creatively. Unresolved grief can be very harmful. It may be compounded with confusion, guilt, fear and isolation and can lead to physical illness. Psychologists tell us that unresolved grief is by far the major source of psychological suffering with which they have to deal.

We can be greatly helped in our passage through grief if we have some understanding of it in advance. Understood and wisely managed, it can be survived without scars and can deepen the quality of our lives. Learning about the process of grieving can open the way to resolving grief from the past. An understanding of grief enables us to respond wisely to the grief of others, a response often sorely lacking in a culture that tends to be embarrassed by pain and grief.

My Own Experience with Grief

Again, I refer to my own life for experience in depth. In my teens I lost, through cancer, a beloved aunt who had cared for me from infancy. Sadly bereft, I meditated deeply on life and finally decided that the best thing I could do for her was to carry on her life. Not necessarily her habits or her ideas (I didn't always agree with these) but the quality of her life, which was characterized by integrity and a profound human dedication. After that my grief went away. As Dr. Leroy Bowman would have pointed out, I found relief by identifying with the person who had died.

In my wife's death the bereavement was more profound. Together, over a period of forty years, we had homesteaded, raised a family, built a business, published a newspaper, presented concerts, run political campaigns, conducted summer work camps and founded a school. Together we had biked, canoed, camped and climbed mountains. Without her my life was suddenly empty. I worked through this in several ways, and over a period of years.

For me perhaps the most important form of release was in personal involvement. I helped take care of my wife before she died, helped lift her body into the box, which we then loaded into my old station wagon. I then drove this myself to the burying ground, helped lower the box and recited her favorite poem about death. Generally, anything that survivors can do to care for the body or assist in services after death will help bring meaning and healing to the experience of bereavement.

A day or so after my wife's burial, we held a large memorial meeting at the school, attended by family, students and friends. At this meeting I spoke for an hour and twenty minutes, telling of my wife's life. This did me a world of good. A few days later we held another meeting, at Yellow Springs, Ohio, where we had lived most of our lives. Again, I spoke, but this time for only forty minutes! Men, in our culture, are denied ready access to tears, and speaking may provide emotional release instead. The importance of this often is overlooked because women usually outlive their husbands and we unconsciously tend to assume that survivors are women.

Before and immediately after my wife's death I was able to respond to the emotional challenge of the situation. The major test was to come later, when the ceremonies were over, the obituaries filed, the family and guests dispersed and life again flowing in normal channels. I knew that unless special measures were taken I would become ill. So, as quickly as possible, I set forth on a business trip, which would involve me in a tight schedule, associating closely with people. My health soon stabilized.

I well remember my return from that trip. It was dusk, and as I drove down the mountain road toward home I thought sadly, "Elizabeth won't be there." The house was dark and I felt lonely. Then I phoned the school, which was nearby. "Are you having All-School Meeting tonight?" I asked. "Yes," they replied.

"How about holding it at my house?"

Sure enough, a few minutes later students and staff arrived, filling the big music room, and a warm sense of fellowship came over me. Clearly, one needs continuing emotional support, sometimes for a year or more.

One aspect of bereavement that I had not anticipated was the loss of identity. With Elizabeth gone I was no longer me! After forty years of sharing on such a broad spectrum of life, I did not have a separate identity. This loss of identity was not painful or distressing, nor did it interfere with my activities. But it was very strange, and several years were required to get over it. I understand this is more often experienced by men, whereas women are more inclined to feel deserted.

Happy involvement with the students and staff of the Arthur Morgan School, work in projects of absorbing interest, and interesting intellectual pursuits soon restored to me a sense of well-being. I had opened myself to grief, had sought involvement, had found ways to express my feelings and had reached out to others. It seemed that I had handled my bereavement well. Actually, I had— but there was still work to be done.

My wife kept appearing in my dreams. She wasn't dead after all—she had merely been away— It seemed so real that the happiness of her return would linger for a time after I awoke. Clearly I still had a long way to go.

Some seven years after her death an incident occurred to change that picture. I found myself attracted to a young woman colleague who embodied some of Elizabeth's qualities. I had no idea of marrying this woman because of the age difference, but the attraction continued. I finally realized that I was, in effect, projecting my wife onto her—trying, in a sense, to use her to bring back Elizabeth. Clearly, I had not yet let go of my wife. This awareness brought a breakthrough in my understanding. I finally did let go of my wife, and my attraction to the young woman subsided to the level of a cordial friendship.

This resolution took time and effort, and I needed to talk freely with someone. My daughter, who had helped me with her mother's care, served as my confidante. Wise and sympathetic, she listened sensitively, saying little. That was what I needed. After seven years I was once again on solid ground.

So, many years after Elizabeth's death, at age 77, I did marry again, very happily, a woman of my own age whom I had known in college, and who like myself had been widowed. We share the same values and concerns. The marriage is a new one, not the reincarnation of an old one.

In contemplating this marriage the problem of death gave me serious pause. I had been married to a wonderful woman, who had died. I was happy again. Did I really want, at my age, to become vulnerable to death once more? The odds were one to one that she would die first—and before many years passed. Conversely, I might die first. During my marriage with Elizabeth there was always the shadow of a fear that I might die, thus deserting her. With her death, this shadow vanished. Having seen her safely across the bar, I no longer feared death. Did I really want to give hostage to life again? But finally I, and my new love, made peace with death and agreed to a marriage which would be temporary—until one of us died. We have deliberately accepted grief as part of life, and are happy.

Group Support in Bereavement

Group support is important in helping to care for a dying person at home. It is also important for a family experiencing bereavement.

It was a beautiful Sunday morning in 1966. I was in Ohio, on the phone with my wife in North Carolina. Suddenly an operator broke in with an emergency call from Detroit. Our younger daughter, age twenty-nine, had been killed in a motor accident.

First I called back to my wife and broke the news to her. That was the hardest part. We set up plans for her to fly to Ohio. Then I phoned one of our friends, who was a member of the Friends Meeting (Quaker), asking him to get the word to the other Meeting members.

At 11:00 a.m. I went to Meeting. Not much was said, but I could feel the love and support. I still remember the words of a thoughtful young man who spoke. "Until we have learned to accept death we are not really living." I found this a comforting thought.

Later I met my wife at the airport and brought her home. As if by magic meals appeared, chores were done and errands run. Old friends came to see us. Hospitality was arranged for relatives from out of town. A memorial meeting was quietly arranged. We seemed to be carried along on a gentle wave of love. We never learned who coordinated that—probably several people helped.*

The memorial meeting was a heart-warming affair, at which several people spoke, all spontaneously.

Looking back on that period, I am struck by the contrast between that occasion and one that had occurred fifteen years earlier, when we experienced another death in the family. On the earlier occasion the members of the Meeting had been sympathetic, but there was no concerted move to help us at a time when help was needed. What had happened to change the situation so much for the better?

For one thing, the Meeting had established a committee to organize help for families at a time of death. From this had grown the habit of doing that, to the point where it happened almost spontaneously. The fact that I turned to the Meeting for help was probably important also. The habit of organizing immediate help for a family at a time of death is practiced in many religious groups. It is a good one to cultivate.

Another thing I would like to stress is the importance of visits by friends following a death. I recall an incident when my wife and I planned to visit a good friend whose husband had died, but were a bit slow in getting to it. When we finally did, she met us at the door, exclaiming, "I *knew* you'd come!" The bereaved person normally has feelings of insecurity and often of guilt as well. The attention of friends is very important. Simple communication of the feeling of caring is probably the most important thing that can be done in the first hours or days after a loss. When the survivor feels like talking or expressing feelings, the listening and acceptance of a friend will help understanding and healing to emerge from within.

Children and Grief

Children, too, experience grief in a form depending on their age and circumstances. Efforts to protect children from grief by explaining death as sleep or a journey can result in serious confusion. The natural anger often expressed by children at the loss of a sibling, parent, grandparent or friend may be shocking to adults. Earl Groll-

*Arrangements for immediate cremation were made through a quick call to the Detroit Memorial Society. Memorial societies throughout the U.S. and Canada reciprocate in assisting one another's members. See Chapter VII, "Memorial Societies."

man's *Talking About Death* (see Bibliography) gives useful guidelines for helping children deal with their anger, sadness and guilt. The pain and anger of a bereaved child may be expressed in nightmares, inability to concentrate, moodiness, uncharacteristic roughness or violence. Children need an opportunity to acknowledge and express the complex feelings of bereavement. They may need help, too, in understanding the grief responses of their parents. Sometimes it helps for a family member or friend to explain to school personnel what is happening.

The Death of a Child

The grief experienced by parents when a child dies, especially if the death is sudden, commonly has a corrosive effect. The anger that is so frequent and normal a part of grieving often is directed against each other. Likewise, intense regret, guilt and blame, loss of the future embodied in the child and sudden inability to continue the caring and nurture in which a parent's life is invested combine to prolong and intensify grief and produce frustration, misunderstanding and stress. The help of a counselor experienced in grief counseling or a group of bereaved parents is usually needed to maintain a stable marriage. It's best to begin such help as soon as the death is anticipated, even when there appears to be no problem. To locate parent groups, see listings in Appendix II.

Conversely, with understanding, the grief can help illuminate their lives, helping them to become more loving and patient. I know a father who loved his children but was somewhat rough with them. Losing one through drowning, he suddenly realized what they meant to him and became kind and gentle.

As a boy I lost a baby sister through the Sudden Infant Death Syndrome. It was totally unexpected, and a great shock to us. Before the baby was taken away, my parents and I stood with our arms around each other—looking at the baby. That was a precious moment, filled with grief and love. The death of a child can draw a family together in warmth and tenderness.

The death of an infant before or shortly after birth is also an occasion for grief. Both parents should be encouraged to see the child, perhaps name him or her, and accept the reality of the child as a member of the family who has died. Not to do so generally results in a partial denial of the death, which may last for years. Friends can help by acknowledging the event by words or caring gestures.

Loss of a child through abortion or adoption needs also to be mourned by mothers, and often by fathers, too.

The National Funeral Directors Association suggests that parents can be helped by "considering holding/dressing/casketing of the infant," as well as by "developing meaningful rites and rituals that involve the parents, grandparents and siblings as participants and not mere observers."[1]

Suicide Survivors

Those bereaved by a suicide are often called "survivor victims" because of the intensified guilt, anger and social stigma that they experience. Healing depends on the realization that the roots of suicide are complex and no one, including parents and spouse, should be blamed. For a discussion of suicide prevention, see Chapter V, "The Right to Die." See also Appendix II for support group listing.

When Someone Causes a Death

How do you comfort a person who has accidentally killed someone? Such a person is normally overwhelmed with feelings of guilt and needs comforting. What do you say or do if you yourself have accidentally killed someone else? How do you behave toward a person who has accidentally killed someone you love?

These are tough questions I never thought about until I confronted them in my own life. That happened when my younger daughter was killed by a drinking driver.

The first thing I did, of course, was to break the news to my wife. This was hard, and it took her a few moments to regain her composure. What she said then was very wise and very characteristic of her. "We must go to Detroit at once, to help the other family!" That, as it happened, was not practical, for reasons of time and distance.

The principle, however, was sound. Had the accident occurred nearby, especially if one of their members had been injured, a visit to express *our* sympathy with their sense of guilt ("We know how badly you must feel") and our wishes for their recovery would have been therapeutic for us and for them.

The man who killed our daughter wrote us a letter, telling us how terribly he felt. This was helpful to us and to him. Thinking about it afterwards, I know I should have responded, saying I realized how he must be feeling and that he must be sharing our grief. Feelings of guilt are a genuine and often devastating form of grief.

Reflecting on this matter, I think if I killed someone in an accident I would take or send flowers to the family and tell them how terribly I felt. I believe both they and I would then feel better. It should be borne in mind that the *legal responsibility* for an accident is not always clear, and a sincere expression of regret need not be formulated in such a way as to accept or deny such responsibility.

What can you do if a friend is involved in a fatal accident? You can visit him and tell him you understand how badly he feels and that you sympathize both with him and with the family that suffered the loss. "It could have happened to any of us."

Emergency and disaster personnel also need to give attention to the emotional needs of persons involved in accidents—and to their own emotional reactions as well. (This concern is touched upon also in Chapter I, Death Education.)

Phases of Grief

Grief and mourning are not unique to death, but occur in many situations of separation, loss or failure. Manifestations vary with different people and may include the following phases, which different people will experience in different ways and in varying sequence—sometimes shifting back and forth.

1. Denial, shock, numbness—delaying realization of the magnitude of the loss—especially in the case of sudden loss.
2. Emotional release—often a flood of tears, realization of loss, beginning of healing.
3. Depression, loneliness, isolation.
4. Physical symptoms—wide variety of digestive, respiratory, hormonal, cardiovascular ailments—you name it! Can be life-threatening.
5. Panic, when a person feels unable to cope with an unknown future, or that there is something wrong with her/him.
6. Guilt, ranging from the almost universal sense of one's shortcomings to the intense guilt often experienced on the death of a child, or when there were unresolved conflicts, or in the case of suicide.
7. Anger, at the deceased for dying, or at anyone who might be

blamed for the death, or at God. This is a normal reaction which is difficult to face and to share.

8. Need to talk, to express feelings, share memories, to find meaning in the person's life.
9. Taking positive actions in response to a death—like working to avoid similar deaths for others, reaching out to persons similarly bereaved, completing projects of, or on behalf of, the deceased. This is always healing, but especially helpful for relief of guilt.
10. Readjustment, reaching out in new relationships and experiences.

Support Groups and Professional Help

Bereaved people often find peer support groups of great help in dealing constructively with their loss. Such groups exist for widows, parents who have lost newborns, infants or older children, and survivors of suicide and murder. Support groups are listed in Appendix II. Books and pamphlets for the bereaved are available from these organizations and some are listed in the Bereavement section of the Bibliography in Appendix I.

A bereaved person may get stuck in some stage of grief. Professional help is probably needed if a person remains in one stage of reaction for longer than three months (in the case of an expected death) or six months (with a sudden death) without some progress being seen.

Avoid the Use of Drugs

Tranquilizers are sometimes prescribed for persons in grief. This may be helpful as a temporary measure, but numbs feelings and tends to prevent the "grief work" which must be done. If medication is more than temporary, professional counseling should be sought.

How Death Illuminates Life

Grief, well handled, sometimes may illuminate life in a very fine way. "When someone you love dies, your love doesn't die, it gets redistributed." My father made this comment late in life on the occasion of a memorial service for a young woman.

His own life was eloquent testimony to this. My mother, reportedly a lovely and talented young woman, died of typhoid fever when I was a few months old. My father and I went to live with his parents and his older sister, who became my foster mother for the first six years of my life.

Sorely bereft, my father directed much of his affection toward me and I enjoyed an almost idyllic childhood. Nor was I the only beneficiary, as my father grew into a warmer and more caring person. He did not seek to avoid grief but by turning his emotional energies outward was able to make his grief a creative force in his life. In a profound way my mother's death illuminated our lives.

It can be helpful for the survivors at a time of death to be aware of this potential and to draw strength and comfort from it. No one lives a full life without the experience of suffering. Whether one withers inside and is crippled by it, or reaches out and grows with it, depends in large part on their own understanding.

Catastrophic Loss

Individual responses to loss can be multiplied in social upheavals to become powerful social and political forces. As an administrator of refugee relief in the Middle East, responsible for 25,000 homeless people, I became acutely aware of the grief they felt. The loss of home, country, livelihood and sometimes of family members as well, represented great bereavement. Many clung to denial, fantasizing return to the homeland. There was a vast reservoir of bitterness and anger against those who were blamed. Terrorism, nationalism and warfare grow, in part, from these collective grief responses.

Life after Death

Many people find solace in the concept of life after death. The continuity of biological life is obvious. Also evident is the continuity of cultural patterns and values. The continuity of the individual soul is an article of faith with most major religions of the world, and each has well-developed ideas on the matter. References for further study are included in Appendix I.

REFERENCE

[1] National Funeral Directors Association, "Sudden Infant Death," 1981.

IV / THE RIGHT TO DIE

This chapter discusses the right of patients to refuse treatment, and the importance and methods of advance planning. It discusses suicide and suggests how to communicate effectively with potential suicides. It discusses the issue of assisted suicide, offers ground rules for self-termination, and speaks out against life-denying habits which account for most self-destruction. It discusses the issue of keeping alive defective infants by surgery and urges that compassion and common sense be used in making difficult decisions of principle.
— Ernest

The Right to Refuse Treatment

This issue has been given a new dimension by continuing advances in medical technology which, in the name of life-saving, commonly prolong the process of dying, often at great cost in terms of suffering and expense. A principal issue is the right and ability of a dying person to remain in charge of what is done to his or her body, choosing when to fight for life and when to be allowed to die. The cost of futile death-prolonging treatment is another major concern. One study showed that forty percent of an average American's total lifetime expense for medical care will be spent in the last thirty days of his or her life.[1]

In common law, the right to privacy gives a mentally competent adult patient the right to refuse treatment at any time, whether for religious reasons, difference of opinion, or mere whim. Only legal minors or those judged unable to make a valid decision are subject to state intervention to insist upon treatment. Violation of a patient's expressed decision is grounds for charges of assault and battery.

In practice, however, families and physicians may override a patient's wishes for a variety of reasons. Families may be unable to accept the death of a loved one and to let the person go, or to risk the guilt of failing to do everything possible for the dying person, or simply to agree among themselves as to the best course of action. Medical personnel then fear legal action should they honor the patient's wishes and override any member of the family. In reality, according to the Rev. John J. Paris, S.J., there has been only one suit on record, either criminal or civil, for discontinuance of life support for a terminally ill patient, and the charges were dismissed.[2]

Hospital personnel and procedures are focused on keeping people alive. To permit a death which could have been postponed may seem a failure, a violation of regulations, or unethical. Intensive care begun under pressure of an emergency becomes difficult for family and physician to discontinue. Under these circumstances, a patient who wishes to refuse treatment is too often regarded as unruly and is restrained or drugged to make him or her more tractable.

It is of utmost importance to discuss these matters in advance and to record decisions in writing. This allows family members to anticipate and adjust themselves to possibilities in advance, and to make peace, if not total agreement, with the dying person's wishes. Because this is a difficult topic to introduce, most physicians will appreciate the family's raising it so that the doctor, too, may come to terms with the patient's desires, and be clear as to the wishes of the family.

A good form for this is the "Living Will" (illustrated in Appendix V), specifying limits to treatment for terminal illness. The Living Will is now legally recognized under the Natural Death Act, or right-to-die law, which has been enacted in thirteen states and the District of Columbia and has been proposed in many more states. Copies may be obtained from organizations listed in Appendix II.

In addition, forty-two states have laws authorizing a "durable power of attorney." This empowers a designated person to make medical decisions for a patient in the event he or she becomes incapacitated. Many Living Will forms include this provision. A separate Durable Power of Attorney form is available from the Hemlock Society, listed in Appendix II.

When completed, copies of the above forms should be given to family members, to your physician, and (very important!) placed in your hospital chart on admission to a hospital.

There is increasing support for the idea that the lives of terminally ill patients should not be prolonged by extraordinary measures unless the patients themselves wish it. This refers especially to "bodily invasion," such as cardio-pulmonary resuscitation, respirators, pacemakers, dialysis and incidental surgery. For example, the Veterans Administration recently joined many other public and private hospitals in making provision that doctors may issue "do not resuscitate" or "no-code" orders for terminal patients under certain conditions, if the patient agrees or, in the case of incompetent patients, if the next-of-kin agrees.

Major Jewish and Protestant groups have taken a position similar to that of Pope John Paul II that, when death is imminent in spite of medical care, it is permissible to withhold treatment that would only secure a precarious and burdensome prolongation of life.

What about life support systems that are not considered extraordinary, such as artificial feeding and antibiotics for persons in irreversible coma? Perhaps they should be withheld also under the above conditions. The American Medical Association recommends discontinuing life support for terminally ill persons in irreversible coma. A survey of Chicago area physicians who dealt with terminally ill people found that ninety percent of physicians approved of passive euthanasia.[3] Ninety-seven percent of nurses polled in a recent survey felt a patient's wishes to discontinue treatment should be honored.[4] These figures appear to be representative of the mainstream of medical opinion. Judgment may be required, too, in the treatment of a reversible illness that occurs along with a terminal one. Pneumonia, "the old man's friend," is an example.

In the United States, more than 5,000 people are being kept alive in what physicians describe as a permanent vegetative condition—totally dependent on intravenous nourishment and medication. Minimal cost of care for each person is estimated to be $75,000 per year. A Presidential Commission on Medical Ethics recommended in 1983 that family members or other surrogates, as well as doctors and hospitals under certain conditions, be allowed to decide for or against continuation of life-prolonging care for patients in irreversible coma.[5]

While the principles may seem clear, many problems arise in carrying them out. It is not always clear when a condition is terminal or irreversible. Families and physicians need to be alert, too, to contradictory feelings in the patient who expresses a wish to be allowed to die. Temporary depression, unmet emotional needs, and exaggerated fear of treatments sometimes enter in and should be considered before a decision is made.[6]

Here again, advance thinking and planning will be of help. By way of reference, I offer my own living will along with the usual version in Appendix V.

A Personal Message

The following letter was written by an elderly physician.[7]

> To the Editor: As one who has had a long, full, rich life of practice, service, and fulfillment, whose days are limited by a rapidly growing, highly malignant sarcoma of the peritoneum, whose hours, days, and nights are racked by intractable pain, discomfort and insomnia, whose mind is often beclouded and disoriented by soporific drugs, and whose body is assaulted by needles and tubes that can have little effect on the prognosis, I urge medical, legal, religious and social support for a program of voluntary euthanasia with dignity. Prolonging the life of such a patient is cruelty. It indicates a lack of sensitivity to the needs of a dying patient and is an admission of refusal to focus on a subject that the healthy cannot face. Attention from the first breath of life through the last breath is the doctor's work; the last breath is no less important than the first.
>
> Consent by the patient with a clear understanding of this act, by the patient's immediate family, by the family physician, lawyer, minister, or friend should violate no rules of social conduct. There is no reason for the erratic, painful course of the final events of life to be left to blind nature. Man chooses how to live; let him choose how to die. Let man choose when to depart, where, and under what circumstances. The harsh winds that blow over the terminus of life must be subdued.
>
> Frederick Stenn, M.D.
> 1240 West Park Avenue
> Highland Park, IL 60036

The Deformed Infant

The prickly issue of withholding treatment from seriously deformed infants has come to the fore through the case of "Baby Jane Doe," born with severe deformities, both physical and mental, who would have died without corrective surgery. The anguished parents with the doctor's agreement, asked that she be allowed to die. The law intervened, ordering surgery. The case has been surrounded by controversy.

On the basis of information in the media, I find myself siding with the parents and physician. Requiring, against the wishes of the parents, that a severely deformed child be kept alive, who would in the course of nature have died shortly after birth unless severe surgery were used, seems to me a misapplication of the principle of respect for life. Parents faced with an agonizing decision of this sort are likely to experience great frustration, grief and guilt, whichever way they decide. In general it seems fitting for the rest of us to support them lovingly in their decision—not to make the decision for them.

It is important, where difficult issues of this sort are concerned, that sensitivity, compassion and goodwill are exercised, along with common sense, and that principles not be applied in a rigid way.

The Problem of Suicide

Suicide is a large and growing problem among young people in our country. Each year more than 5,000 people under the age of twenty-four are known to commit suicide in the United States and experts assume that a significant number of deaths recorded as accidents are actually suicides. When one adds unsuccessful suicide attempts, ten percent of students in high school and college may be at risk of suicide.[8] And the problem is getting worse. Among adolescents, suicides doubled between 1970 and 1980.[9] Hence suicide is a delicate topic that frequently comes up in discussions of death.

One responsibility of the teacher of a class in Death Education—or of any teacher—is to be sensitive and alert to the need for help on the part of any student. An occasional death wish is experienced by most normal people. When this becomes a preoccupation it can sometimes be observed by strong statements such as "death is peace, or reunion," or "suicide is a reasonable alternative." Inability to concentrate and recent excessive use of alcohol or drugs also may be warning signs. It is good, when possible, to have an experienced counselor present at sessions when the subject of suicide is on the program.

On Communicating with Potential Suicides

I had a letter once from a woman I had never seen, who had a terminal illness and wished to cut it short. She said that none of her friends or family would talk with her about it, and asked if I would correspond with her—which I did. Exchanging letters, we discussed the pros and cons and the various ramifications involved. I neither encouraged nor discouraged her. After a while she decided, on philosophical grounds, that she would rather stick it out and let nature take its course.

When a person says, "I think I'll kill myself," we should listen not just to the words, but to the feelings behind the words. He or she may really be saying, "I'm very unhappy." For us to say, "Come, come, now. Don't talk like that!" is more likely to stop further communication than to change his or her mind. If we can accept the statement without challenging it ("Yes, it must be very hard for you," whatever the trouble is), the person will have a chance to ventilate his or her feelings.

One recent study showed that ignoring or rejecting someone's expressed desire to die was more likely to result in actual suicide.[10] Conversely, allowing a patient to openly discuss suicide results in a decreased likelihood of suicide.[11] Accepting what a person has to say and giving sympathetic moral support can have a healing effect and help restore the person's will to live.

Then, too, paradoxical as it may seem, when a person "decides" to commit suicide, it sometimes makes him or her feel better and begins a process of emotional recovery. Encourage such a person to talk, and listen thoughtfully. Commonly it is the one who doesn't talk who is in the greatest danger.

A doctor in my family, when asked by patients to help end their lives, would tell them which medicine, if taken all at once, would be lethal. The sense of empowerment that this gave to the patients, who no longer felt helpless, apparently helped restore the will to live. None of them took the medicine.

Ground Rules for Self-Termination

While strongly disapproving of suicide in most cases, I would point out that a rule intended to prevent one form of tragedy, if arbitrarily applied, may lead to other and worse forms of tragedy.

I hold that, for the terminally ill, the deliberate ending of one's life is sometimes a good and wise act. Since the word suicide carries overtones of tragedy and disgrace, it may be helpful to use a less judgmental word to apply to wise self-termination. I am concerned here with the difficult task of formulating principles to govern the decision for or against self-termination.

1. The decision to end one's life should rest with the person in question, and the means for doing so should be in his/her hands.

2. A decision to end one's life should *never* be carried out at a time of depression or despair. Likewise, pathological motives, such as a desire to hurt someone, should be guarded against.

3. Pain control should be double-checked. People are sometimes driven to suicide by chronic or unbearable pain that could have been relieved.

4. Drastic disability or incurable illness may be grounds for ending one's life. An elderly doctor, learning that he had an incurable cancer, determined to enjoy fellowship with his family to the fullest during his remaining months of life, and then, at the onset of his final decline, and with their consent, quietly end his life with an appropriate drug. Thus he would spare himself and them the pain and expense of going the hard way. The family agreed and their last months together were deeply happy. His death did not involve suffering and his family, while they experienced grief and loneliness, did not suffer from shock or a sense of guilt.

5. One's social role and relationships should be taken into account. Being a living burden on a loving family may be better than leaving and may be less burdensome than the feelings experienced by the survivors following the commonly misunderstood act of "auto-euthanasia" (suicide). This is an individual and family matter. The conservation of social resources may be considered, too— energy, money and medical resources.

Helping Someone to Die

A man I knew, in the final stages of cancer, asked his friends to bring him a drug with which he could end his life. This they did, but being very conscientious and wishing to be aboveboard, they notified the authorities about what they were doing. The sheriff's deputies rushed to the scene, but too late—the man was dead. No action was taken against the friends.

There have been many cases of mercy killings. Compassionate doctors and family members undoubtedly do it more often than we know. One young man even honored his mother's request to shoot her in the hospital. A number of people have been brought to trial for such actions, but, so far as I know, few have been convicted and none have been imprisoned after being convicted.

Thus we have a dilemma. Is it better to let "assisted suicide" remain outlawed, and then be humanely discriminating in enforcing the law, or to change the law itself? There is something to be said on both sides. This matter is dealt with in depth by The Hemlock Society, which can provide counsel, information and literature. (I am a member of this society.) The Canadian Law Reform Commission Working Paper, "Euthanasia, Aiding Suicide, and Cessation of Treatment," available free, is a good discussion of legal considerations. See Appendix II for addresses of these and other organizations.

"Respectable" Forms of Suicide

No thoughtful discussion of suicide is complete that does not make reference to people who kill themselves a little every day. While society deplores "sudden suicide," it ordinarily condones the "slow suicide" implicit in a wide range of life-denying habits. Heart disease, for instance, our number one killer, can be greatly reduced by wholesome eating, appropriate exercise, avoiding overweight and steering clear of tobacco. The second killer, lung cancer, in 88% of cases is attributed to smoking. The third killer, automobile injuries (about 50,000 deaths per year in the U.S.) can be greatly reduced by the use of seat belts and even more by non-drinking. Jellineck's disease (alcoholism) afflicts some twelve million people in the United States. It is said to shorten life by ten to twelve years and is involved in 50% of all auto accidents, 80% of home violence, 30% of suicides, 60% of child abuse and 65% of drownings. Its economic cost is calculated at $54.1 billion annually. It is difficult to cope with because most sufferers firmly deny they have it.[12] The fourth killer, cirrhosis of the liver, is also associated with drinking.

The fifth killer, strokes, is commonly related to excess weight, as is hypertension, which is a frequent cause of strokes. Venereal disease is making a frightening comeback. The Center for Disease Control reported a sharp increase in syphilis in the U.S. in 1980, and *The New York Times* reports gonorrhea as the most common bacterial disease of humans, with an estimated fifty million cases worldwide. Even worse is herpes, which has assumed almost epidemic proportions and for which there is no known cure. All of these can be prevented.

The widespread excess consumption of sugar and caffeine also is conducive to degenerative disease. The annual per capita consumption of sugar in England is reported at 120 pounds, and the U.S. is close behind. Heroin and other drugs claim thousands of lives and diminish the quality of life of thousands more.

Increasingly, also, the pollution of our environment is taking a toll of life and health.

In short, self-destruction is rampant in our society. Why do people indulge in life-denying habits and needlessly dangerous acts? Is it in part because they do not accept the reality of death? They think they are defying death, whereas they are actually denying it. It is commonly the person who has been most careless in his or her habits who, when the chips are down, clings most desperately to the shreds of life. Those who have lived fully and are at peace with their lives can most easily face death, including the choice of a time for its ending.

REFERENCES

[1] *Yankee* magazine, "Man at the Crossroads," May 1984, p. 167.

[2] *Ibid.*, pp. 168-9.

[3] R.G. Carey, and E.J. Posavac, "Attitudes of Physicians on Disclosing Information to and Maintaining Life for Terminal Patients," *OMEGA*, 9:67-76 (1978), quoted in *Sourcebook on Death and Dying*.

[4] *Nursing Life* magazine poll of 3,000 nurses, Jan/Feb and March/April, 1984.

[5] *Yankee*, op. cit. p. 72.

[6] David L. Jackson, and Stuart Youngner, "Patient Autonomy and 'Death with Dignity': Some Clinical Caveats," *New England Journal of Medicine*, 301:8, pp. 404-408 (1979).

[7] Quoted with permission from *New England Journal of Medicine*, 303:15 November 9, 1980, p. 891.

[8] Michael Peck, "Youth Suicide," *Death Education*, 6:1, Spring 1982, p. 29.

[9] Carl Tishler, Patrick McHenry and Karen Morgan, "Adolescent Suicide Attempts: Some Significant Factors," *Suicide and Life Threatening Behaviors*, 2:2, Summer 1981, p. 26.

[10] Jonelle Timlin, "Study Shows Most Counselors Favour Change in Euthanasia Laws," in *Hemlock Quarterly*, Jan. 1983.

[11] S.L. Dubovsky, "Averting Suicide in Terminally Ill Patients" in *Psychosomatics*, 9:2, pp. 113-115, 1978.

[12] *Newsweek*, October 17, 1983.

V / SIMPLE BURIAL AND CREMATION

This chapter discusses funeral costs and how to control them; how to get dignity, simplicity and economy in funeral arrangements. It discusses the options for body disposal, the values of simplicity and the importance and methods of planning. It discusses financial planning and financial resources at time of death, with reference also to prepayment plans and legal arrangements. It cautions against swindlers. It outlines things to be done at time of death, and tells about funerals conducted without funeral directors.

For critical help in preparing this chapter I am indebted to Howard Raether of the National Funeral Directors Association, Friend Deahl and Marcia Goldberg of the Continental Association of Funeral and Memorial Societies, and my daughter-in-law, Vicki Morgan, who chairs the Burial Committee of the Yellow Springs Friends Meeting. — *Ernest*

The commercialization of death in our culture has resulted in expensive and ostentatious funerals. In 1982 the average "total adult" funeral cost was $2,138[1] plus another $1,250 for earth burial and trimmings,[2] making a total of $3,388 for getting one body underground.

We heartily agree with funeral directors that death ceremonies, wisely planned, are important in meeting the social and emotional needs of the survivors. (See Chapter VII, Death Ceremonies.) We would add, however, that the amount of money spent on such ceremonies generally has little to do with how well they meet those needs. Just the same, families who want expensive services and are prepared to pay for them should get what they want.

Why Are Most Funerals So Costly?

Funeral directing is an honorable and necessary business, but it is in a unique situation. About 22,000 funeral homes in the U.S. handle about two million deaths per year, an average of about ninety-one each. However, a tiny fraction of the funeral homes handle a majority of the business; thus many have less than one funeral per week. How do the thousands of morticians survive whose plants are idle more than eighty percent of the time?

Some have other sources of income. Many, however, manage because they can and do charge the overhead of days and weeks of living expense and idle plant to a single funeral. This is possible because competition does not exist in their business in the same way it does in other businesses.

Mark Twain puts it neatly, with an undertaker saying:

> There's one thing in this world which a person don't say—
> "I'll look around a little and if I can't do better I'll come
> back and take it." That's a coffin. And take your poor man,
> and if you work him right he'll bust himself on a single lay-
> out. Or especially a woman.

Most bereaved relatives, in a state of shock and grief following a death, see no alternative to accepting what a funeral director presents as proper and acceptable. He, in turn, is naturally concerned as a businessman to sell sufficient services to meet his expenses.

Regulation of the Funeral Industry

This situation has naturally led to abuses, and these were dramatically brought to public attention in 1963 by Jessica Mitford's *The American Way of Death.* Even in 1983 the U.S. Senate Special Committee on Aging rated these abuses among the top ten most harmful frauds directed against the elderly.[3]

In the U.S., the federal and state governments and the funeral industry itself have all taken steps to curb these abuses and improve industry practices. In particular the Federal Trade Commission, after years of study, public hearings and legal appeals by industry groups, approved a consumer protection rule requiring itemized price disclosures by funeral directors before arrangements are made, including price disclosure by telephone. The FTC rule prohibits common misrepresentations of legal, crematory and cemetery requirements and any suggestion that embalming, caskets or burial vaults can preserve a body for a long time. Unfair practices, such as embalming without permission, requiring a casket for direct cremation and requiring purchase of unwanted merchandise, are forbidden. The rule must be reviewed after four years to determine if it should be amended or terminated.[4] Individual states have additional consumer protection laws. A survey of these laws is available from the Continental Association of Funeral and Memorial Societies.

There is often confusion about state laws. Some funeral industry practices are required by law, some are not; and funeral directors are not always sure which are which. Hence they are sometimes mistaken in the legal information they give to clients.

Laws governing the care and disposition of human bodies are meant to protect public health and safety, but sometimes their purpose is to promote the interests of the funeral industry. For example, some states have a law that only a licensed funeral director or "direct disposer" may transport a dead body. Several require embalming under certain circumstances, such as length of time between death and burial and availability of refrigeration.

Funeral directors, like other business groups, have active lobbies in most state and provincial capitals. Most of the state boards that regulate the funeral industry are composed of funeral directors. Regulations made by these boards acquire the force of law. Such regulations usually pertain to qualifications of funeral directors, building requirements, etc., more than to consumer issues. These regulations tend to be variably interpreted and enforced, depending on local conditions.

It is important in this, as in other industries, that the regulatory boards contain a majority of non-industry members and provide for full representation of the consumer viewpoint. It is important also that memorial societies and other consumer organizations be alert to legislative developments affecting funeral practices in order to be able to initiate legislation in the interest of the consumer. Ways and means of doing this are discussed in some detail in the *Handbook* for memorial societies, prepared by the Continental Association.

Where to Go with Complaints

In 1982 the National Funeral Directors Association, in cooperation with the U.S. Office of Consumer Affairs, established a consumer action panel, ThanaCAP, to arbitrate consumer complaints. Funded by the NFDA, the panel is staffed by recognized consumer advocates who meet periodically to hear complaints submitted jointly by consumers and funeral directors.

This action panel did not become fully functional until May, 1983. In the ensuing five months it completed arbitration of twelve cases. From every indication it would appear to be a genuine and sincere effort on the part of the funeral industry to prevent and correct abuses. It has suffered thus far from lack of recognition by the media, which has limited its usefulness. It is to be hoped that appropriate use will be made of the panel, so that it can demonstrate its capacity to serve.

It should be borne in mind that the reluctance or unwillingness of certain funeral directors to provide simple services at low cost does not constitute an abuse, but instead is a problem to be addressed by memorial societies.

If a funeral director is unwilling to submit a complaint for arbitration, the consumer may address the state licensing board (c/o the governor, if the address is not known) sending copies to the state attorney general's office and to appropriate consumer protection agencies at the local, state and national levels.

What Are the Options for Body Disposition?

The following options are listed in approximate order of cost, with the least expensive first. There is a great deal of variety within most of these options, which will be discussed later.

1. Immediate removal to a medical school, followed by a memorial service. (See pages 147-148 for instructions.) Generally this avoids all expense and performs a valuable service. There can be a brief gathering of the immediate family before removal if circumstances permit, but this must be done quickly.
2. Immediate cremation, followed by a memorial service. (See "About Cremation," p. 51.) There may also be a commitment service at the crematory chapel if desired.
3. Immediate earth burial, followed by a memorial service. There may also be a graveside commitment service if desired.
4. A funeral service in the presence of the body, followed by removal to a medical school.
5. A funeral service in the presence of the body, followed by cremation.
6. A funeral service in the presence of the body, followed by earth burial.

The preceding alternatives assume the services of a funeral director, except possibly in cases of immediate removal to a medical school or for cremation.

Burial at sea is an option if circumstances permit.

Burial by the family, or by a committee or a religious organization is sometimes an option. (See "Non-Professional Funerals," page 55.)

What's the Difference between Funeral and Memorial Services?

A funeral service is, by definition, a service held in the presence of the body. The casket may be open or closed. A memorial service is a service held after the body has been removed. Both serve the same purpose. Each has something to recommend it. A discussion of the two types of services will be found in Chapter VII, Death Ceremonies.

The Practice of Simplicity

Simplicity in arrangements can effect great economy, but even more importantly it can help center attention on spiritual values and the life of the person who has died, rather than on material things. It can avoid the appearance of ostentation and extravagance.

In general it is in the removal and disposition of the body that close family members are helped to recognize and accept the person's death. Appropriately, the ceremonies that follow the death are best focused on the life of the one who has died, and thus help start the healing process.

In the case of "immediate removal" it is often good for the closest family members to be given an opportunity to accompany the body to its destination and to help load and unload it. If burial is used, they may accompany the body to the graveside and start the filling of the grave. There may be a small commitment service at the graveside or crematory if desired. This may include a prayer, poem or song, as desired. The main commemoration, however, would be either a funeral service (before) or a memorial service (after). If the family owns a suitable vehicle, that should be used for conveying the body—not a hearse—and a family member should be encouraged to drive it. Always provide ample opportunity for family involvement. This is easier if arrangements are simple. (See Chapter VII, Death Ceremonies.)

The Need for Planning

Simplicity doesn't happen by accident. When death occurs in a family in which there was no planning, the survivors find themselves virtually helpless in the face of entrenched custom and dealing with a funeral director who expects them to follow this custom. Through planning, however, a family can have the precedent, information and moral support needed to get the type of service it wants.

Thousands of Families Being Helped

To help with advance planning, non-profit funeral and memorial societies have been formed in some two hundred cities in the United States and Canada with a membership of over one million. These societies cooperate with funeral directors, sometimes by having contracts with them and sometimes by advising their members as to which firms provide the desired services. They also assist those who wish to leave their bodies for education or their eyes or other tissues for transplant or therapy. (See Chapter VI, Memorial Societies.)

If No Memorial Society Is Near

How near must a society be? Some societies cover just one town. Some have connections with, or information on, funeral directors in several states. Much depends on the kind of services wanted. A long haul may be economical if the body does not have to be brought back for a funeral service, as when a memorial service is used.

Planning without a Society

The simple arrangements and low rates obtained through a memorial society can generally be had by anyone. To find a cooperative funeral director, however, and to make such arrangements without embarrassment, is likely to be difficult. Sometimes a church, labor or fraternal group can function on behalf of its members. In such cases it is good to keep participation open to non-members and to look forward to becoming a full-fledged memorial society.

The family should talk the matter over and decide whether cremation, burial or medical school is preferred, whether there shall be viewing of the remains, and whether a funeral or memorial service is wanted. These are the main decisions. Then visit various funeral directors, explaining your wishes, and see what each has to offer. This should be done while the family is in good health. It is unfortunate that many people are unwilling to accept the reality of death in their own families and find it difficult to plan ahead. A memorial society helps to overcome this.

Planning Helps Understanding

Advance planning is needed, not only in making arrangements with funeral directors, but for working out understanding within the family. A young man killed in an accident left a widow and young children with no savings. Both husband and wife believed in simple burial, and the widow was fortunate in getting a funeral director who encouraged her to carry out her desire for a simple and economical arrangement. The young man's mother, however, though unable to help with the expenses, insisted on an elaborate funeral. Since there had been no advance planning, the wife was unable to resist and not only had to endure a ceremony distressing to her; but had to face life with small children, her husband gone and a heavy funeral debt hanging over her. More explicit planning might have avoided this unhappy outcome.

Persons wishing to leave organs or tissues to aid the living, or who wish to leave their bodies to a medical school, have a particular responsibility to reach an understanding with their families ahead of time.

Write It Down!

A valuable help in planning is a four-page form called "Putting My House in Order," which is available from the Continental Association of Funeral & Memorial Societies (See Appendix VII). Plans for body disposition and death ceremonies, as well as financial and property records, can be indicated on this form. A similar, though less comprehensive form called "Preparing Today for the Eventual Tomorrow" is available from the National Funeral Directors Association. (See Appendix II.) Do *not* include funeral plans in your will, as wills are seldom read until after the funeral.

Simplicity Without Pre-Planning

If you desire simplicity and economy but are confronted with a death in the family without advance plans, there are still alternatives, though not as easy. First of all, consider the options listed on p. 44.

If you opt for immediate removal to a medical school, consult the Directory of Medical Schools in Appendix IX to determine which, if any, medical schools within a reasonable radius are in need of bodies, then phone the Anatomy Department there.

If you prefer some other alternative, check to see if there is a memorial society in your area (see Directory in Appendix VII). Call the society. It may be too late to join, but, in any case, the volunteer will take a personal interest and give you as much advice, moral support and information as possible. Some societies will accept members at this time.

If this can't be arranged, the thing to do is to ask some knowledgeable friend, perhaps your clergyman, to help you locate a cooperative funeral director and to go with you to see the funeral director and help make arrangements. Your friend can ask questions without embarrassment and can give important moral support. Bear in mind that funeral directors are often skilled merchandisers who downplay their cheaper merchandise. Don't be put off if the funeral director refers to a simple service as a "welfare funeral."

It is entirely proper to ask about prices, and FTC rules now require funeral directors to provide such information in person or over the phone on request. An itemized price list of services and merchandise must be presented before arrangements are made. A funeral director may no longer require you to purchase a "package," as was mostly done in the past.

Financial Resources at Time of Death

Social Security Death Benefits are available under some conditions to the survivors of persons who were covered by Social Security. These benefits must be formally applied for. Those eligible for the Social Security lump sum death payment of $255 are:

1. A surviving spouse living with the covered worker at time of death.
2. When a spouse survives who was not living with the covered worker at the time of death, such spouse will be eligible for the lump sum payment only if s/he was receiving a monthly benefit on the deceased's record during the month of death or would have been eligible for such benefit if an application had been filed for it.
3. If there is no surviving spouse, a child will be eligible for the lump sum payment if s/he was entitled to or eligible for Social

Security monthly benefits on the deceased's record during the month of death of the deceased worker.

Union and Fraternal Benefits are provided by many trade union and fraternal organizations to the families of their members. Many such benefits go unclaimed each year because families are unaware of them. Such possibilities should be checked promptly by the family. Also, there are benefits for the survivors of any man who has ever been a railroad employee. Some of these benefits are availabe only for funeral expenses.

Insurance and Employee Benefits. No family needs to be told to file claims for life insurance. Often, however, there are other forms of insurance, depending on the circumstances of the death, which provide benefits for the survivors. If occupational factors were involved in the death, Workman's Compensation Insurance may be in effect. There may be automobile club insurance. In other cases liability insurance of one kind or another may be invoked. The families of state employees in some states are entitled to survivor benefits. Such possibilities should be checked. Incidentally, burial expenses for indigent families are commonly paid by the county.

Benefits for Veterans include death benefits for veterans who served in the U.S. Armed Forces during World Wars I and II, the Korean War, the Vietnam War and certain peacetime service, if they have not been dishonorably discharged.
- A burial allowance up to $1,100 will be paid when a veteran dies as the result of a service-connected disability.
- A sum up to $300 plus transportation costs will be paid where the death of a veteran occurs in a VA facility. The transportation allowance will be within limits prescribed by the VA.
- When death does not occur in a VA facility, the payment of the $300 burial and funeral expense benefit will be made in the case of a veteran who was receiving a VA compensation or pension benefit or who would be deemed to have been so entitled if evidence on file on the date of death was sufficient to support a determination of entitlement.
- A veteran can be buried in a National Cemetery (transportation costs paid under certain circumstances) and receive a government headstone or marker for a grave in a government or other cemetery. Some national cemeteries also have gravesites, garden niches or columbaria available for cremated remains. In lieu of

burial in a government cemetery, a $150 plot allowance will be made. An allowance toward the purchase of a marker in lieu of a government headstone/marker is available.

Families of veterans also may be eligible for ongoing financial assistance in the form of monthly survivor benefits. Your local Social Security and Veterans Administration offices and your funeral director can assist you in obtaining these benefits.

Protection through a Credit Union. Many, but not all, credit unions have an arrangement whereby deposits made before age fifty-five are doubled (not to exceed $1,000 or $2,000) at time of death. In most credit unions, however, if death occurs between fifty-five and sixty, 75% of savings are matched; between sixty and sixty-five, 50%; between sixty-five and seventy, 25%; and after seventy, none.

Thus a person under fifty-five, by making a savings deposit of $500, creates a death benefit fund of $1,000 but still receives interest on the $500 savings and can withdraw them at any time.

Another arrangement is to borrow the $500 from the credit union and deposit it as savings, thus creating a $1,000 death benefit fund. When the loan is paid, interest will accrue on the savings. If the loan is not paid, it will be cancelled by the credit union at time of death.

Either of the above arrangements is an entirely legitimate and businesslike way of covering burial expenses for any member of the family. But check first with your credit union to make sure they offer the desired services.

Life Insurance. Many families carry a small insurance policy on each member for the specific purpose of meeting burial expense in case of death. In such cases, the family should decide in advance what type of services are wanted and what they are likely to cost. Otherwise the expense may be several times the anticipated amount. Just as inflation makes life insurance a poor form of savings, so it makes it a costly way to provide for death expenses—though better than none.

Mutual Aid Plans. Some groups, including a number of Mennonite Church congregations, assess each family when a death occurs.

A "Totten Trust" is a savings account in your name to which is added "in trust for ..." the relative or friend who is to use the funds as you direct. It may be in a credit union, bank or other savings institution.

Funeral Prepayment Plans

These are offered by various enterprises, including some funeral directors and others calling themselves "cremation associations," "pre-need associations" and such. These plans involve a form of trust which, in most states, is legally required to be refundable, or largely so. A summary of state laws regulating such trusts is available from the National Funeral Directors Association.

Most of the businesses offering these plans are reputable. In general, however, we advise against such plans, in view of the complexities and uncertainties of modern life—inflation, moving, business failures, etc. There are commonly better alternatives. Whatever procedure you choose, be sure to keep the funds under your control.

About Cremation

Modern cremation is a clean, orderly process for returning a human body to the elements. Ordinarily it is economical, too. With the rising cost of land burial and, in some areas, shortage of land, it is finding increasing use. Many prefer it for aesthetic reasons.

In just the last ten years cremation increased in the United States from 7.66% of deaths to 12%, with fewer cremations in the southeast and midwest and up to 40% on the West Coast. In Canada the percentage is about twice as high.[5] In England and Northern Europe the rate is over 50%. "Calcination" is similar to cremation, except that the body is exposed to intense heat, rather than flame, and similarly reduced to bone fragments and powder.

These "ashes" are clean and white and may be stored indefinitely or mailed by parcel post for distant interment. Some families prefer to scatter them in a favorite garden or woods, from a mountain top, or at sea. (First make sure they are pulverized, to avoid visible bone fragments. This can be done at home if necessary, or, by request, at the crematory.) Sometimes ashes are kept in urns. A few states have laws prohibiting the scattering of ashes. Such laws are commercially motivated and serve no hygienic or aesthetic purpose.

Most religions permit cremation. Roman Catholics may now request permission from their Bishop, and such requests are usually granted. Greek Orthodox and Conservative and Orthodox Jews oppose it, as do some conservative protestant groups, Moslems, and Baha'is.

Crematory charges range from $50 to $200 and occasionally

more. If arrangements are made through a funeral director, his charges for transportation and paper work may run from $50, if handled through a memorial society, to $800 or more if no prior arrangement is made. According to 1982 NFDA statistics, funerals in which cremation was the final disposition cost $2,165, whereas funerals in which earth burial was the final disposition cost $1,292, though neither of these figures included crematory or cemetery charges.[6] The cost for cremation can be greatly reduced if there is no public viewing and a simple wood or corrugated container is used for the body. Many funeral directors can provide these inexpensive containers if requested.

In some places religious groups or private citizens may obtain the necessary death certificate and transportation permit and transport a body directly to the crematory, usually provided no one is being paid. (See "Non-Professional Funerals," p. 55.)

In recent years a new and useful service has appeared in many areas, through which a body may be removed and cremated immediately after death, without embalming, at low cost. Since the services of a trained funeral director are not required, some states now license "direct disposers" as a special category. Some organizations offering direct cremation call themselves "societies," apparently to capitalize on the goodwill of memorial societies. This is not accurate; all the ones we know are commercial ventures and should be described as "services." Some are operated by mortuaries. Some have contracts or agreements with memorial societies. Most of those who do not have connections with a memorial society charge rates above those available through memorial societies. You can find out about this by contacting your local society and comparing costs and services.

Earth Burial

This is still the most common form of body disposition in the U.S. and Canada. "Traditional" cemetaries allow families to select any gravestone they like; "memorial parks" require that the stones be level with the ground. Simple markers cost a minimum of $250 plus engraving.

Prices for grave plots vary from about $150 to $600 or more. Opening and closing a grave costs $300 or more, with an extra charge for weekends or holidays. Concrete grave liners are required by most cemeteries to prevent the ground above the grave from subsiding with time. Concrete or metal vaults may also be used as grave liners; some are guaranteed waterproof for a period of years and costs range up to $1,500 and more.[7] Some of these are sold with the dubious claim that they will preserve the body. Actually, decomposition may occur at a faster rate because a complete seal promotes the action of anaerobic bacteria on the body. Some people choosing earth burial prefer that their bodies return to the earth in a natural manner, and therefore use wood or corrugated boxes.

In some rural areas religious groups handle burials in their own cemeteries at minimal cost. (See "Non-Professional Funerals," p. 55.) In some states burial is permitted on individually owned land or in family burying grounds by the family, religious group or funeral director.

Transportation of Bodies

Sometimes a body needs to be transported for a ceremony or interment in a distant place. If a common carrier is to be used, a funeral director will be required and will know what to do. Before using air express, check with AMTRAK. It offers quick service to many destinations and is much cheaper than air.

If the body is to be transported by the family in a suitable vehicle, a transportation permit can be obtained from the Health Department. This requires a death certificate signed by a doctor. Depending on the weather and the distance to be traveled, embalming or dry ice may be needed. This matter can be talked over with the Health Department. With the appropriate transportation certificate, state lines offer no problem.

The handling of transportation by members of the family can be emotionally wholesome, and can effect a large economy, too.

Death in a Foreign Country

Some 8,000 American die in foreign countries each year. Anyone going abroad should carry in his passport instructions to be followed in the event of death. This should be done regardless of age or good health and discussed with families before leaving home, to avoid conflicting instructions. A second choice should be indicated, in case the first choice should not be available. The full name of father, maiden name of mother, full(maiden) name of spouse, date and place of birth and occupation should be listed. If the person has a will, the exact location should be included, along with the name of the executor, if any.

If someone dies abroad while accompanied by an adult member of the immediate family, that family member will make the arrangements. The nearest American consular office should be contacted and can give helpful advice. If no adult family member is along, the consular office is responsible to notify the next of kin in the United States, and then carry out their instructions concerning disposition of the body. The consul will furnish to the next of kin a "report of death" which has the legal status of a death certificte. The consul is also prepared to serve as "provisional conservator" (not administrator) of the deceased's property in the foreign country. A small percentage fee is charged for this.

In any case, advance payment in full is normally required for disposition of the body. If instructions and/or payment is not received in a reasonable length of time, the consular office allows local authorities to dispose of the body as unclaimed.

Cremation, in countries with facilities for it, is normally the least expensive method of disposition. If cremation is not available in the country where death occurred, it may be available in a nearby country. Costs vary greatly. In the Sudan a cremation costs $60, in France, $1,500. Ashes may, if desired, be sent home by mail.

Earth burial is universally available and varies greatly in cost. In some countries it may be cheaper than cremation. In most countries (Moslem countries tend to be exceptions) bodies may, if desired, be exhumed and returned home after six to twelve months. In many countries burial grounds are re-used after a period of several years and the family will receive notice that the remains are to be removed and placed in a common grave area.

Often bodies of people who die abroad are flown home. This requires embalming, which is not always readily available, plus special packing and a hermetically sealed coffin plus an outside shipping case. This adds up to several thousand dollars. Consulates usually know which mortuaries are able to handle such complex shipments. Obviously, disposal of the body in the foreign country can save a lot of money, and even there great differences in cost are likely to be found. If you prefer the cheapest way, be sure to say so. Don't hesitate to "shop around."

Non-Professional Funerals

A scattering of groups and individual families care for their own dead without the assistance of a funeral director. They are found mostly but not entirely in rural or semi-rural places. A few are religious groups such as the Quakers or Mennonites. Others are rural families, particularly in Appalachia. Some are organized within the framework of a memorial society. Royal Keith, a former president of the National Funeral Directors Association, said on the television program "Over Easy" that any individual can take a body to to a crematory or bury it without the services of a funeral director so long as the legal requirements are met—however, opposition based usually on misunderstanding may be encountered. These requirements govern death certificate, transit permit, authorization to cremate, filing with proper authorities, time lapse between death and disposition, proper grave site and body container. Requirements vary from state to state. Crematories and cemeteries may have rules of their own as to how bodies may be brought to them—for instance, whether or not a vault or grave liner must be used.

Any group or family who wish to care for their own dead need to understand the role of the coroner. His responsibility is to check on accidental deaths, homicides, suicides and sudden or unexpected deaths, especially when no physician had been in attendance. It is mandatory that all such deaths be reported to him promptly. Illegal abortions also fall within his province as do cases of stillborn infants when there is suspicion of some illegal action. In short, it is his job to officially determine the cause of death and whether there has been foul play and to prevent unjust accusation of the innocent. He should be given active cooperation. A friend of min, a Christian Scientist, died without benefit of a physician. His family wished to handle arrangements without a funeral director but didn't realize they needed a death certificate from the coroner. This got them into some embarrassing difficulty.

One local group which has successfully cared for its own dead for many years is the Yellow Springs, Ohio, Friends Meeting (Quakers) which has its own burial committee. Member families wishing to sign up with the committee fill out forms in advance, authorizing the committee to act on their behalf, and include the necessary biographical data and endorsement by the next-of-kin. (The form is shown in Appendix VI.)

At time of death, or when death is expected, the first action of the group is to assist the family in a coordinated way. Immediately after death a member of the committee gets the death certificate signed by the attending physician or coroner and takes it to the Health Dept. (or appropriate state agency) to be recorded. The committee keeps blank death certificate forms on hand. In some states a transportation permit must be obtained at the appropriate state agency. The next of kin signs an "authorization to cremate" and makes out a check to the crematory. Burial or removal to a medical school follows much the same pattern with appropriate authorization from next of kin. Members serve without pay, which minimizes the possibility of legal complications. At the same time that the care and disposition of the body are being handled, other committee members assist the family with food, baby-sitting, hospitality for relatives, getting out death notices, etc., and helping to plan a suitable memorial service. This support is very meaningful.

This committee and its arrangements did not come into being overnight. Members of the committee had examined the laws and had explained their plans carefully to the state Department of Health and to the local Health Department. They set up advance arrangements with a crematory and visited each of the nearby hospitals so that there would be no misunderstanding or delay when they had occasion to function.

An example of a simple burial conducted on a non-professional basis was on the occasion of my wife's death. The burial committee of Celo Friends Meeting quietly functioned. Friends and students at the Arthur Morgan School quickly built a box from materials already at hand and cut to size. They dug a grave in the Friends' Burial Ground, arranged a graveside committal service followed later by a memorial service and assisted the family in various other ways. The whole thing was beautifully handled, conveying a warm feeling of fellowship and support. My total cash expense was $23 for plywood plus a $2 filing fee.

What to Do when Death Occurs, if a Funeral Director Is Used

A doctor or coroner must declare the person dead and sign a death certificate, which can be obtained from the hospital, health department or funeral director.

When the family is ready to have the body taken away (see Chapter II, "Living with Dying"), the funeral director of their choice is called. The hospital or nursing home will do this for you if the death has occured there. Memorial society members will call a cooperating funeral director (often listed on a wallet membership card), who may have a copy of the family's arrangement wishes and will know exactly what to do.

This applies to most memorial societies. Some, however, have no cooperating funeral director and operate only in an advisory capacity. Such societies can suggest to the family which funeral director to seek, and what services to ask for. This, too, can be very helpful.

A clergyman, appropriate church or synagogue committee or friend should be contacted promptly to help the family in such ways as are needed, and especially in making arrangements with the funeral director if there has been no advance planning. (See pages 47-48.)

Checklist of Things to Be Done

(You may wish to tear out or photocopy these pages and attach them to your plans for final arrangements.)

☐ Arrange for members of family or friends to take turns answering door or phone, keeping careful record of calls.

☐ Coordinate the supplying of food for the next days.

☐ Arrange appropriate child care.

☐ Decide on time and place of funeral or memorial service(s). (See page 76.)

☐ Make list of immediate family, close friends and employer or business colleagues. Notify each by phone.

☐ If flowers are to be omitted, decide on appropriate memorial to which gifts may be made (such as a church, library, school or charity).

☐ Write obituary. Include age, place of birth, cause of death, occupation, college degree(s), memberships held, military service, outstanding work, list of survivors in immediate family. Give time and place of services. Deliver in person or by phone to newspapers. Some papers charge for death notices.

☐ Arrange for hospitality for visiting relatives and friends.

☐ Consider special needs of the household, for cleaning, etc., which might be done by friends.

☐ Select pallbearers and notify them. (See page 71.)

- ☐ If deceased was living alone, notify utilities and landlord and tell post office where to send mail. Take precaution against thieves, especially during the time of the funeral/memorial service.
- ☐ Plan for disposition of flowers after funeral (e.g., hospital or rest home).
- ☐ Prepare list of persons to receive acknowledgements of flowers, calls, etc. Send appropriate acknowledgements. (Can be written notes, printed acknowledgements or some of each.)
- ☐ Prepare list of distant persons to be notified by letter and/or printed notice, and decide which to send each.
- ☐ Prepare copy for printed notice if one is wanted.
- ☐ Notify lawyer and executor. Get several copies of death certificate.
- ☐ Check carefully all life and casualty insurance and death benefits, including Social Security, credit union, trade union, fraternal, military, etc. Check also on income for survivors from these sources.
- ☐ Check promptly on all debts and installment payments. Some may carry insurance clauses that will cancel them. If there is to be a delay in meeting payments, consult with creditors and ask for more time before the payments are due.

Planning for Inheritance—Keeping Down Legal Costs

Survivorship can be enormously simplified if the person who has died has taken the trouble to discuss these financial matters with his or her family and make appropriate plans. Failure to do so can lead to conflict and much unnecessary work and expense.

Everyone who owns property should make a will, carefully determining what he or she wants to do and paying a competent attorney to draw up the document. If a person dies without a will, his/her property will be distributed in accordance with state law, often not at all what the person would have chosen. An executor to administer the estate also should be selected in advance. If not provided in the will, an executor will be appointed by the court.

Careful estate planning may also minimize state and federal inheritance taxes and probate costs. There are many legal instruments for doing this, and tax laws frequently change. It is therefore advisable to consult an attorney to make one's plans. In 1984, federal inheritance taxes were charged on estates over $340,000, with projected annual increases in this minimum.

Chief Justice Warren Burger once commented that standard legal fees charged to probate an estate after a death are frequently out of proportion to the value of the services rendered. These fees are in some cases well earned; in others they constitute a sheer windfall. Justice Burger remarked that the legal profession had allowed the "relatively simple business" of settling a will to "become encrusted with excess procedural baggage that...often adds unreasonably to costs." Often a percentage of the value of the estate is charged, regardless of the amount of work involved. While it is wise to use an attorney in these matters, a family may minimize legal fees by handling many of the details that usually take up much of the attorney's time, using the attorney in an advisory capacity and to handle the more technical matters. All records concerning finances, property, insurance, etc., should be kept in good order and readily accessible, as attorneys often spend much expensive time straightening out records. See "Write It Down," page 47 for sources of forms to simplify record keeping.

It is entirely proper to negotiate an agreement with an attorney whereby the attorney will charge for the time spent. $50-$75 an hour under present conditions is not unreasonable. Better yet, arrange a flat fee for the job. Sometimes an experienced accountant can handle the entire process. For such work, especially if the accountant is a CPA, s/he should receive a comparable rate of pay.

Beware of Vultures

Survivors, particularly widows, are commonly preyed upon by swindlers of one kind or another. A favorite device is to collect a nonexistent debt owed by the deceased, or to deliver merchandise (commonly a Bible) that was never ordered.

Another ploy is to inform the survivor of a non-existent life insurance policy on which a final premium must be paid before benefits can be collected, or of some other valuable asset requiring a final payment of some kind.

Widows are prime prospects for bad investments and even reputable investment firms, when asked, will sometimes recommend changing stock portfolios merely for the sake of the commissions involved.

The moral is, be careful, go slow and consult an experienced member of the family or other trusted business advisor.

REFERENCES

[1]National Funeral Directors Association survey, 1983, from "Facts About Funerals," NFDA, 1983.

[2]*Forbes Magazine,* September 26, 1983, p. 178.

[3]"Information Paper," June, 1983.

[4]Federal Trade Commission, "Funeral Industry Practices: Trade Regulation Rule," *Federal Register,* 47:186 (9-24-82).

[5]*The Cremationist,* Apr-May-June 1980, and *Forbes,* 9-26-83, p. 178.

[6]*Statistical Abstract of Funeral Service Facts and Figures of the United States,* 1983 edition.

[7]"Planning a Funeral at a Fair Price," *Changing Times*, Sept. 1980, reprinted in *Sourcebook on Death and Dying,* edited by James A. Fruehling (Chicago: Marquis Professional Publications, 1982), pp. 145-146.

VI / MEMORIAL SOCIETIES

No discussion of death education, of hospice, or of simple burial can be considered comprehensive which does not include a report on memorial societies. Memorial societies constitute the most important lay movement of our time relating to funeral practices and death ceremonies. A directory of funeral and memorial societies in the U.S. and Canada will be found in Appendix VII.

As author of the "Manual of Simple Burial," I was invited in 1963 to attend the founding meeting of the Continental Association of Funeral and Memorial Societies and served for many years on its board of directors. The "Manual" has served as sourcebook and advocate for the memorial society movement since its inception. My daughter, Jenifer Morgan, who collaborated in editing this edition, is a former Executive Secretary of the Continental Association. — Ernest

What They Are and How They Work

Memorial societies are cooperative, non-profit consumer organizations, democratically run, that help their members to get simplicity, dignity and economy in funeral arrangements through advance planning. They are not run by funeral directors.

These societies themselves generally do not offer funeral services but act in an advisory capacity and often have contracts or agreements with funeral directors on behalf of their members. Thus they help their members to get exactly the services they want, and at reasonable cost. The work of the societies is done by unpaid volunteers in most societies; a few of the larger societies have paid secretaries.

Memorial societies do collectively what few individual families are prepared to do—they inquire around, compare services and prices, then share this information with their members. They do *not* collect payment for funeral services. (For information on alternatives for the disposition of bodies, see Chapter V, "Simple Burial.")

Memorial Services

In addition to advising their members on funeral arrangements, these societies can often help with suggestions for memorial services. (See also Chapter VII, Death Ceremonies.)

A Million Members

There are memorial societies in some 200 cities in North America, with a combined membership of more than one million people. Most societies charge a one-time membership fee of $10 to $25, and some have a small "Records Charge," which they collect from the family at time of death, via the funeral director. They effect large savings for their members and are an outstanding example of how consumers, by democratic group effort, can empower themselves at the grassroots level.

Membership Is Transferable

Families moving to another city can transfer their membership at little or no charge. Likewise when a death occurs away from home, the society in the host city, and its cooperating funeral director, will assist the family.

History

The practice of group planning for funeral arrangements started early in the century in the Farm Grange organization in the northwestern United States. From there the idea spread to the cities, mainly under church leadership. The People's Memorial Association of Seattle, organized in 1939, was the first urban group. Organizations spread gradually up and down the West Coast, then eastward across the United States and again northward into Canada.

Continental Association of Funeral and Memorial Societies

By 1963 the societies had become a strong continent-wide movement, and the Cooperative League of the U.S.A. called a meeting at Chicago, where Canadian and U.S. societies together formed the

Continental Association. (The member societies, and literature a-
vailable from the Association, are listed in Appendix VII.) The Association serves as a central clearinghouse for information and
publicity and assists new societies in forming. In several states
where there are a number of societies, state federations have been
organized to follow consumer issues within the state and to act as
needed.

Having a strong central office, the Association is the principal
consumer advocate for the funeral industry. In this capacity it
speaks not only for its immediate membership but for the 221 million Americans who are not members, all of whom must someday
die. Working closely with the Federal Trade Commission, it was instrumental in securing passage—after a long struggle—of legislation requiring funeral directors to quote prices freely and to offer
their services on an itemized basis, rather than as package deals.
This does not tell people what kind of funerals they should have, but
broadens their opportunity for choice and opens up important savings. The Association recently conducted a nationwide education
project, funded by the government, directed at assisting the elderly
to cope with funeral problems.

The Memorial Society Association of Canada

In 1971 the Canadian Association was formed, in close collaboration
with the Continental Association. It performs in Canada essentially
the same functions as those performed by the Continental Association in the U.S. Together the two associations include nearly all the
bona fide memorial societies in North America. (See Appendix VII
for the names and addresses.) A notable exception is the Memorial
Society of British Columbia, with seven branches and 120,000 members. As we go to press, its membership in the Canadian Association is in process.

How to Organize a Memorial Society

An organizational *Handbook for Funeral and Memorial Societies* is
available for $3.50 from the Continental Association. In addition,
the Association has "area coordinators," persons experienced in
memorial society organization, who are located in various parts of
the country and are often able to give a hand in helping new societies to get started.

Financial Savings

Memorial society members commonly save fifty to seventy-five percent of usual funeral costs, with total savings to members of millions of dollars annually. In 1983 the People's Memorial Association of Seattle, the largest society in the U.S., had a contract for funeral service and burial at $480, to be compared with an average cost for a "total adult" funeral of $2,138.[1] For the ninety-eight percent of PMA members electing cremation, the contracted price is $280. An average of about 1,000 services are provided to PMA members annually, helping to make funeral costs on the West Coast the lowest in the U.S. These savings resulted in part from collective bargaining but more from the simplicity that members are encouraged to practice.

Cooperation with Funeral Directors

In many cases, memorial societies negotiate contracts or agreements with funeral directors through which the society members can get the services they desire, and at predetermined prices. While many funeral directors take a dim view of memorial societies, arrangements between funeral directors and societies generally have proved satisfactory to all concerned.

In cases where no contracts or agreements can be arranged, memorial societies are generally able to advise their members where to turn to get the services and prices they want. In a couple of cases, where funeral directors refuse to cooperate at all, the societies have found ways to by-pass them altogether.

The Social Base of Memorial Societies

By and large it has been prosperous, educated, middle-class families that have organized memorial societies—doctors, lawyers, teachers, business people. Mostly they have been church people, too, and mainly concerned with simplicity. Ironically, working-class families and minority ethnic groups, on whom the burden of funeral costs falls most heavily, have been less inclined to join memorial societies.

Memorial society leaders have been concerned with this and have kept the doors of membership open to all. Some societies actively seek members and leadership from minority groups and the less affluent, with modest success in recent years.

Imitation "Societies"

The success and popularity of memorial societies have led to imitations. Private companies, calling themselves societies, have entered the funeral service business in various places. Some offer "direct cremation" service. This is a valid form of disposition of human remains, but it is misleading for such firms to call themselves "societies."

If someone from a "society" tries to sell you something or offers you a prepayment plan, investigate carefully. Memorial societies have no commercial interests and rarely charge membership fees over $25. In general, memorial societies advise against prepayment plans. There are various ways to make advance financial provision for death. (See pages 50-51.)

Nearly all bona fide societies in the United States and Canada are members of either the Continental Association or the Memorial Society Association of Canada. When in doubt about a society, check in the directory in Appendix VII to see if it is a member.

REFERENCE

[1] National Funeral Directors Association survey, 1983, from "Facts About Funerals," NFDA, Sept. 1983.

VII / DEATH CEREMONIES

This chapter deals with the various social and emotional needs of survivors at a time of death, and how death ceremonies can help meet these needs. It discusses also various options available in death ceremonies in our culture and some of the characteristics of each, with special attention to memorial services.

It includes listing and description of components which may be used in planning a memorial service. In Appendix VIII are several examples of memorial services, followed by selected readings appropriate to such services.

The main work of preparing this chapter was done by Ann Baty, of the Bowling Green Memorial Society, who studied the subject over a period of years and corresponded about it with hundreds of clergy and lay people. Valuable ideas and understanding were derived also from the work of the late Dr. LeRoy Bowman, whose book "The American Funeral" remains an authoritative source after 25 years. Some details are drawn from my own experience, with the hope of livening the text.

—Ernest

Humankind, from earliest times, has practiced death ceremonies and procedures in great variety. The reason for these ceremonies is not hard to understand. Such procedures are important to the healing process. No human being lives in a social vacuum; our speech, habits, values—the very meaning of life—derive from our association with one another. Hence the death of one individual is traumatic for the survivors. Recognizing that death ceremonies and related customs are important in meeting the social and emotional needs of the survivors, we should plan these ceremonies carefully.

It has been said that in recent years there has been a worldwide move towards de-ritualized funerals (and other ceremonies, too). Our purpose in this section of the *Manual* is not to weaken or eliminate ritual but to help create more meaningful rituals.

Needs to Be Met by Death Ceremonies

Every situation is different, with different circumstances, different personalities and different needs. Here are some of the needs that are commonly found, and ways in which appropriate ceremonies can help meet them.

Re-establishing Relationships. Death, like marriage, changes a broad range of relationships, as between parent and child, brother and sister, and friends. After a death in the family we are not quite the same people we were before. We therefore must rediscover ourselves in a new set of relationships. This relates directly to the process of mourning.

A promising child of a prominent family had died suddenly, to the great shock of the family and community. A simple service had been held, with just the family and a few close friends. Then for days afterwards, as the mother encountered other good friends, each felt the necessity of conveying sympathy, at the expense of unhappiness to themselves and of rubbing fresh salt in the wounds of the poor mother.

Had the service been open to all, in quarters large enough to receive the friends, the individual condolences could have been replaced by a single meeting, the relationships re-established, and life could have been resumed in a more normal way.

Identification. The ceremony can cultivate a sense of identity with the deceased. The survivors can be helped to recognize that they have shared the person's life and that they are now, in their own lives, the custodians of the values that s/he lived by. In a sense their lives can be a memorial to him or her, and with them lies the power to immortalize the deceased.

A young man whose career had been joyously and usefully devoted to human service had died. Entering the church for the funeral service, his stricken parents appeared utterly crushed and forlorn. It is said that the death of a grown child is the hardest to bear.

In the audience were a large number of young people who had known this man and shared his concerns. The speaker talked of the young man's life and what he stood for and went on to say that his ideals and spirit were alive and growing in each of those present. In a very real sense, said the speaker, his effective work was just beginning, and would go forward in the lives of his friends. The response of the listeners could be seen in their faces; most of all, in the faces of the parents. Leaving the church they were almost radiant and one of them remarked, "Wasn't it fine?" Suddenly all these young people had become, in spirit, their children.

Affirmation of Values. It is almost a universal experience that at time of death the survivors are prone to think seriously of the meaning of life and to meditate on its values. They are at that time not only open to inspiration but hungry for it. The occasion, therefore, should be used for the enrichment and refinement of life. This is perhaps the most enduring comfort that can be given.

Relief of Guilt. At time of death the surviving members of the family are commonly torn between their feelings of love and grief, and the shock and revulsion they tend to feel in the presence of the dead body. It is normal, in this situation, for them to recall their short-comings with respect to the deceased and to reproach themselves. No human relationship is perfect. A wife recalls how she scolded poor Henry for tracking in mud. Children remember how they neglected their parents. A husband remembers that Mary never did get that trip to the seashore that she wanted so much. "But it's too late now."

Apparently this is usual. Certainly it is the major basis of many costly and ostentatious funerals.

One of the functions of death ceremonies is to gently and quietly remove this sense of guilt through the process of re-affirmation of values and a profound sense of identification, which asserts the continuity of the personality of the deceased in the lives of his or her family and friends.

Perhaps the strongest force in lifting the sense of guilt is the reacceptance that the survivors experience from their friends. Love and solidarity help greatly. A thoughtfully planned service provides an excellent opportunity to express this.

Rehabilitation. When an old person dies after his or her powers have declined greatly from their prime, it is helpful to the survivors to have the memory of this person redirected to the good years of his or her life. Before my father-in-law died, his mental powers had failed and life had become an unhappy burden. His death produced a mixture of grief and thankfulness accompanied by a certain amount of guilt. There was no viewing of the remains. At the memorial service we brought into focus what he was and did and stood for in the good years of his life. From that day on we carried with us the image of the fine strong person he was during those years. No amount of cosmetic restoration could have taken the place of that. In fact, any viewing at all would have detracted from the desired effect.

Religious Observance. The occasion of death is an important time to deepen spiritual life, draw on the strength of religious experience and tradition, and unify a congregation. Services planned with the family's clergyman and held in a house of worship can help greatly in this process.

Emotional Support. A death in the family is like an amputation. The survivors have lost part of themselves, and experience intense loneliness and insecurity. The gathering of family, friends and community can be a great source of encouragement and strength. This rallying of support, I might add, should not wait for the funeral or memorial service. Family members and close friends should visit promptly.

A State Funeral. On the death of a prominent person with whom many people had a meaningful emotional relationship, there is need for a ceremonial in which large numbers of people can take part.

An outstanding case in which the social and emotional needs of the survivors were skillfully and sensitively met was the funeral of President John F. Kennedy. The casket was not opened for public viewing. There were no truckloads of flowers in the funeral procession. Since the entire nation had a close emotional relationship with President Kennedy, an impressive ceremony, widely televised, in which the whole nation could participate, was in good taste and filled an important emotional need.

Three Types of Death Ceremonies

a *funeral service* is, by definition, a service held in the presence of the body, with either an open or closed casket. A *memorial service* is by definition a service held after the body has been removed. It can be either a substitute for a funeral service or in addition to a funeral serivce. A *commitment,* or *commital, service* is a brief, optional service held at the graveside or in the chapel of a crematory. It is usually in addition to a funeral or memorial service and is the occasion at which the immediate family and possibly a few close friends bid good-bye to the body.

Ministers and funeral directors are trained in conducting funeral and commitment services, but not all have had experience with memorial services. The following pages, therefore, are devoted mainly to memorial services.

First, however, I want to offer a few comments on funeral and commitment services. These have greater possibilities for variety and for survivor participation than usually are realized. They may be programmed closely or may provide for spontaneous participation by the survivors.

Many years ago a young priest in Hays, Kansas read the *Manual* and liked the idea of participation by the attenders at a funeral. Accordingly he designed a model funeral service, which was performed at a national meeting of the Catholic Art Association devoted to the liturgy of death. I took part in that demonstration, which proved to be a skillful blending of Catholic ritual with Quaker sharing of testimony. I recall also an excellent Quaker funeral with a closed casket, at which the funeral director presided and the attenders, including the husband of the woman who had died, did the speaking as they felt moved.

At a funeral, the choice of pallbearers should favor members of the family who may wish to take part. Instead of civic leaders and business associates being called, the family should have the first chance—including women and teenagers. I have known women who felt deeply deprived because they were excluded from this privilege. The less husky pallbearers should be distributed so that they don't have to lift too much. Indeed, if the box is too heavy, it suggests that the family may have been extravagant in choosing it. Remember also to be careful not to call upon persons with serious heart or back problems. There are more such than we commonly realize.

At a commitment service, too, there can be family participation. At my wife's interment I recited one of her favorite poems and helped lower the box into the ground. Family members may be encouraged to start filling in the grave. Such things are emotionally helpful to the survivors.

An important decision to be made in planning a funeral service is the choice between an open or closed casket. It is the overwhelming preference of clergymen—Protestant, Catholic and Jewish— that the casket be closed. In many cases the viewing of the remains is confined to family members and takes place before the funeral. When family members have been with the body at death or soon after, no later viewing is necessary.

A good "memory image," as funeral directors call it, may be created without viewing the body. Personal reminiscences of the living person can usually generate a better image than viewing the "restored" body.

There are, however, times when cosmetic restoration can be helpful, as when relatives from far away wish to see the body. This does not necessarily require a public viewing. Sensitivity to the wishes of the family should be the key to decisions in this matter.

If a service is held with the casket present, it may be covered with a gray cloth (or pall) as is done, for instance, in Episcopal churches. Thus a solid bronze casket carries no more prestige than a plywood box. This symbolizes the belief that we are all equal in death and helps focus on the spiritual significance of the occasion.

About Memorial Services

A memorial service performs much the same function as a funeral service, but tends to have a more positive atmosphere. This is mainly because it is focused on the values of the person who has died instead of on the dead body.

Members of the family should be encouraged—but never pressured—to speak or to offer songs or prayers as they may choose. The following experience is an example of how helpful a memorial service can be, with appropriate family participation.

A friend of mine lost a grown daughter in an automobile accident. He loved her dearly, but there had been some stress between them, and this made her death doubly hard for him. I went to see him and his wife. It happened that I, too, had lost a daughter some time before in a similar accident.

The family were not members of the Society of Friends, but I offered to arrange a memorial service in the Friends Meeting House and suggested that the father might like to speak at such a meeting. They accepted the offer, but he wasn't sure he would be able to speak. However, he called me shortly afterward and said he did indeed want to speak and wanted me to preside.

At the appointed time the meeting room filled with people. It was decorated with wildflowers; on the mantle was a painting done by the young woman. Her former music teacher played a piece that she had especially liked. Then I spoke, saying that we had gathered in the girl's memory and that any who felt moved to speak should feel free to do so. After a few more words I sat down. Then the father got up. In his hand was a bunch of little cards. On each card was a reminder of some incident from his daughter's life, starting from early childhood. He spoke with difficulty at first, but soon became more fluent. As he continued to relate happy memories, a faraway look came into his eyes and he began to smile, and the assembled friends smiled with him.

His wife thought he was speaking too long and tried to catch his eye but their son, seated next to her, said, "Let him talk." And he did, for quite a while. When he sat down there was a period of silence, then their friends began speaking in turn, spontaneously, words of comfort and philosophy and reminiscence. We let the speaking run its course, and by the time the service was over, it was dark outside. We carried a few chairs into the yard and set candles on them. The friends moved freely about inside and outside the building, visiting with members of the family and with each other. That meeting was, as any good funeral or memorial service should be, the point at which the family could begin to resume normal life and look to the future. They expressed the warmest appreciation.

There was an interesting sequel to that meeting. A few weeks later the father had occasion to attend the funeral of a business colleague. It was a strictly conventional service at which the minister delivered a cut-and-dried oration—and that was it. My friend was struck by the contrast between his daughter's service and that of his colleague, and he expressed anger at the impersonal and empty character of the latter service.

Self-Planned Services

Some people like to plan their own services. These may be conventional services at which the person selects the readings and songs and perhaps indicates the persons whom he or she would like to have to do the readings. Some have planned that their family and friends shall simply come together for a social evening in their memory, with refreshments and fellowship. The memorial may take the form of an entertainment provided by the one who has died.

Self-planned services sometimes take odd and unexpected forms. One man decreed that gaiety be the keynote, with funny stories. The man's son led off by telling one of his father's favorite jokes, and the attenders followed through with amusing anecdotes from the man's life. There was much laughter.

People's wishes should be respected, but they can be encouraged to avoid bizarre arrangements. In most cases they will avoid these anyhow.

Multiple Services

It is often desirable to hold more than one gathering, in cases where different groups or distant places are involved. On the occasion of my wife's death, one gathering was held at Celo, North Carolina, at the Arthur Morgan School, another at Yellow Springs, Ohio, where she had spent most of her life. (I spoke at both!)

Sometimes friends or colleagues in a remote place hold a memorial service independently. This should be fully reported to the family, who will take comfort from it.

No Service at All

Is it ever appropriate to have no funeral or memorial service at all? Yes, under some circumstances this is entirely appropriate.

One such circumstance that comes quickly to mind is that the person wanted it that way. An understanding family may, quite properly, comply with that wish.

Recently, a young man was accidentally killed two thousand miles from his parents' home. It had been years since he had lived with his parents. His work kept him moving from place to place and he had lost contact with his boyhood friends, few of whom still lived in the home town. His parents quite properly decided not to hold a formal service. Friends of the family called at their home to express their love and caring.

Bearing in mind that death ceremonies do in most cases help meet an important need, the decision not to hold a service in a particular situation may be entirely appropriate.

Combination Programs

A mixture of programming and spontaneous contributions is often a good arrangement. Commonly the program starts with music while people are gathering. If one or more family members are musicians, it is appropriate for them to play. If no such family members are available, then friends are appropriate. The quality of personal participation is more important than the technical excellence of recorded music. The latter can be used if no musicians are available.

After the opening music an appropriate reading is in order, either poetry or prose. Best of all is some bit of inspirational writing by the person who has died, though this may not be available. A few suitable selections are offered in Appendix VIII.

Following the reading a brief talk may be given relating to the person who has died. This can be followed by more music and another reading. After that, the attenders can be invited to share their thoughts, feelings and memories. When this seems to have run its course, there can be more music followed, if desired, by a prayer. After a period of silence the attenders should be invited to remain to visit.

Ceremonies on the Death of the Very Young

The tragic death of a young child presents special problems because of the greater guilt and anger often intermingled with the family's grief. If the memorial service is handled wisely and with sensitivity, the love the parents had for the child often can be channeled into greater affection for one another and for their surviving children.

If the service is conducted by a minister or other functionary, s/he can help to develop this concept. If the meeting allows for testimony by the attenders, any concerned articulate friend or relative can make the contribution.

The death ceremony for a baby will naturally be less extensive than for an adult or an older child, though it should provide an opportunity for friends to give emotional support. However, there should be a ceremony, if only a modest one.

In the case of a stillborn infant, it is well for the parents to have a small ceremony of their own, very simple, giving the child a name, recognizing it as a member of the family and signalizing its birth and death.

Miscarriages and abortions also generally involve grief. This is a private matter, but again an informal ceremony may be helpful. Here also the understanding and support of relatives and friends is very important in sustaining parents through a bereavement that is often unacknowledged by our society.

How to Plan a Service

Ideally the family should sit down together, along with their clergyman if they have one, and talk it over. Ann Baty describes this well: "you reminisce, you recall things he said, things he wrote, his ideals, his goals, his plans, his affections—even the annoying things he did. You look over old snapshots. You talk about him and you think about him. From these reflections you begin to plan your ceremony of remembrance." This is a wholesome process that can do much to promote emotional healing.

Time

The time usually preferred for a memorial service is the same as for a funeral service—two or three days after the death. Evenings and weekends are preferable so that more people can attend. The timing may be modified to meet individual situations, as, for instance, if some member of the family is in the hospital or too far away to come until later. Additional ceremonies at a later date may be appropriate. After my father's death there were two memorial gatherings, followed seven months later by a two-day convocation in his memory attended by family and colleagues from far and wide.

Place

The place of meeting, too, depends on circumstances and should accommodate the expected attendance. To assemble a handful of people in a large hall or sanctuary is forlorn. To turn people away for lack of space is even worse. A familiar place is good. It may be a church or a living room—or even outdoors.

The Format of a Memorial Service

Here are a few basic components with which a memorial service may be planned and procedures to be considered. A service may be designed to use them in any way the family prefers.

Most religious groups have specific forms of worship for death ceremonies. A family wishing to follow any specific observance will want the assistance of a clergyman of that faith in preparing and carrying our their plans.

Forms and liturgies may be adapted to include many of the following elements and will in turn suggest specific content and adaptation. Most forms of ritual permit greater flexibility and variety than is generally used. Don't be afraid to express your wishes and explore possibilities.

Instrumental Music: While people are gathering, it is often good to have some muted organ music, if in a church, or quiet recorded music elsewhere. Or the attenders can gather in silence and have the service begin with music. In that case, it is good to have live music if that is available. Music by family members or friends is best of all.

I recall a memorial service in my own family, held in a yard beneath the trees, in which by prearrangement the sound of musical chimes from a friendly church (of a different denomination) a few blocks away came through the trees beautifully at just the right time.

Music can be interspersed in the program, too, if desired, or can be used to close it.

Singing: This is a very desirable form of music for a memorial service, since it allows for full participation by family and friends. The choice of songs is, of course, important. Unless the song or songs are well known to the attenders, it is good to have song sheets or hymn books available. If printed or duplicated programs are used, it is sometimes appropriate for the words of the songs to be included.

Solo or ensemble singing can have a place, especially if done by friends or members of the family. Always encourage family participation.

The Presiding Function: One individual, generally a minister or a friend of the family, customarily presides, stating the purpose of the gathering and setting the program in motion. This person may or may not also contribute remarks, readings and prayers. It is commonly he or she who signals the end of the service by rising and greeting the attenders, or by shaking hands with the nearest persons.

As a rule the presiding person sets the service in motion, and the various participants follow one another in prearranged sequence without further action by the presiding person.

In services in which the attenders are invited to take part as the spirit moves them, this is carefully explained by the presiding person at the time when the service is opened to participation by the attenders. This may be at the beginning, as in most Quaker services, or toward the end.

Prayers: For many families, depending on their practice and belief, this is an important part of the service. Prayers may be offered by the minister or other presiding person or by any family member or friend who feels comfortable with this kind of expression.

Biographical Remarks: It is often appropriate to give a biographical account of the person's life at the outset of the service. This adds interest and meaning to the service and provides an opportunity for family participation.

Reminiscences: Whether programmed or unprogrammed, these add greatly to the service and help to convey in depth some feeling of the person's life and values. It is in the offering of these thoughts and rememberings that family members should be especially encouraged.

Sometimes certain family members and friends are asked specifically to contribute their recollections, and these are scheduled in sequence to be the main part of the program. I recall a fine memorial service in which a series of speakers had the same topic: "I remember Charlotte."

Don't avoid humorous reminiscences or incidents that may have involved some frustration. If presented in good taste, these carry overtones of affection and a fuller picture of the person's life and personality.

Films, Slides and Pictures: The use of visual material is sometimes appropriate, when such material is available. A family member, preferably, should do the narrating. A small display of photographs from the life of the person is always appropriate at a memorial service and certainly has advantages over "viewing the remains."

Silence: Though most commonly associated with Quakers, this practice is observed in many groups, with an appropriate period of silence included as part of the service.

Readings: There is a wealth of beautiful and inspiring poetry, prose and scripture to draw upon. The Bible is a rich source. Likewise the writings of Gibran, Tagore and many others. These readings can be programmed or, in the case of unprogrammed services, they can be offered by the attenders. A few selected readings and some helpful sources are listed in Appendix VIII.

A highly appropriate variation on this procedure is to include writings of the person who has died, if available. These may constitute part or even all of the readings.

Unprogrammed Contributions: These may constitute the entire service, following the opening music, a biographical sketch and introductory remarks in which the attenders are invited to speak. Or they may be called for later in the service and have a smaller place— or they may be omitted entirely. It is well for the presiding person to suggest that at least a short period of silence be allowed to elapse between speakings.

Care should be taken that the time for unprogrammed contributions not be cut short. I have known family members who carried regrets for years that they were cut off from speaking because the service was "running too long."

A word of caution: If the attenders are unfmiliar with the practice of unprogrammed speaking, it may be well to have a few people prepared in advance to help get the speaking started.

Visiting After the Service: It is often desirable for the attenders to have an opportunity to visit with the family and with each other informally after the service. It is good if facilities provide for such visiting—as with a pleasant lawn or a spacious room.

Refreshments: The serving of refreshments during the period of visiting is a pleasant practice that tends to facilitate conversation. In some cultures it is a practice to have a meal after the funeral or memorial service. The custom of the funeral feast is well known. In theory this is supplied by the family of the deceased, but in common practice, it is thoughtful friends and neighbors who supply the food and do the work.

Flexibility

Established procedures are often useful, but they should not be binding. One memorial service was held with everyone seated in a circle. At the close of the service they all stood and joined hands to sing a final song together. Another service (for a golfer) was held as a walking party across a golf course, winding up at the club house for refreshments. Another took the form of a reception at the home of the family whose member had died.

Sometimes the family likes to have articles present that remind them of the person who has died. This is especially attractive when it takes the form of craft or art work, but a favorite toy, in the case of a child, or something connected with a hobby or a profession in the case of an adult also may add a touch of intimacy or color.

Printed Programs

Programs are not necessary, but sometimes they are nice to have. If a service is largely unprogrammed, there is no need for a printed program. If it is highly programmed and especially if it involves group singing, then a program, including the words of songs, can be helpful.

Also relevant is the availability of a church mimeograph or other inexpensive duplication facility. If the service is held in a church, and if the church has a supply of attractively printed program blanks, these may be appropriate.

Or the family may wish to spend the time and money to work up a longer program, perhaps with the full text of the ceremony, that can also be used as a death announcement to be mailed to friends of the family who could not attend. This may include a biographical sketch and some personal tributes. At any event there are options, any of which may be suitable.

Remember

Grief has many dimensions, which are experienced by different people in different ways. (See Chapter III, Bereavement.) Likewise death ceremonies take many forms. As Ann Baty says, do not be coerced into passive acceptance of a conventional pattern; do not be afraid to be creative. Remember that death is a natural event and an occasion for the honest expression of your deepest values.

VIII / HOW THE DEAD CAN HELP THE LIVING

This chapter is essentially a tract—an urgent appeal for human solidarity, to persuade people to think in terms of Life and to share with the living any organs or tissues which, at the time of death, they or their loved ones no longer need. To bury or burn organs or tissues needed by the living is a form of blasphemy against life. Let us not be guilty of it. As for myself, I'm leaving my entire body for medical education.

This chapter sets forth the options and the procedures for each. Directories and addresses of organizations will be found in Appendix IX.
— Ernest

Poet Robert Test states the issue beautifully:

The day will come when my body will lie upon a white sheet tucked neatly under the four corners of a mattress, located in a hospital busily occupied with the living and the dying. At a certain moment a doctor will determine that my brain has ceased to function and that for all intents and purposes my life has stopped.

When that happens, do not attempt to instill artificial life into my body by the use of a machine and don't call this my deathbed. Let it be called the bed of life and let my body be taken from it to help others lead fuller lives.

Give my sight to the man who has never seen a sunrise, a baby's face or love in the eyes of a woman. Give my heart to the person who has nothing but endless days of pain. Give my blood to the teen-ager who was pulled from the wreckage of his car so that he may live to see his grandchildren play. Give my kidneys to a person who depends upon a machine to exist from week to week. Take my bones, every muscle fiber, every nerve and try to find a way to make a crippled child walk. Explore every corner of my brain, take my cells, if necessary, and let them grow so that some day a speechless boy will shout at the crack of a bat or a deaf girl will hear the sound of rain against her window.

Burn the rest and scatter the ashes to the wind to help the flowers grow.

If you must bury something, bury my faults, my weaknesses and my prejudices against my fellow man. Give my sins to the devil, give my soul to God.

If by chance you wish to remember me, do it with a kind deed or a word to someone who needs you. If you do all I have asked, I will live forever.[1]

Urgent Need for Anatomical Gifts

There has been a tremendous breakthrough in the past five years in the technology of transplanting tissues and organs due to the discovery, in 1979, of cyclosporin, a new drug derived from a plant. This drug helps patients to accept transplants without weakening their resistance to infection which, in the past, took the lives of many.[2] Hence, transplants are increasing rapidly—both in number and in the variety of organs being transplanted. This, of course, results in vastly increased need for donors. Persons over sixty may contribute corneas, bones, skin and pituitary hormone. Younger persons are preferred for major organs. (The presence of cancer or a communicable disease disqualifies a donor, except for corneas.)

The donation of organs or tissues does not alter the appearance of the dead person at a funeral, nor does it cause him or her the slightest discomfort or inconvenience. The disturbance to the body is generally less than that involved in the routine process of embalming. There is no cost for organ donation—the transplanting hospital assumes costs from the time of death until the removal of the organ. The family is still responsible for disposition of the body.

Following are some of the anatomical gifts that are urgently needed, along with instructions for bequeathal. (See also Appendix IX.)

Bequeathal of Eyes to an Eye Bank

Eye donations are increasing, but the demand is increasing even more and in some areas is reported as "desperate." Age and condition of the body, except for the presence of leukemia, are no obstacle to donation of corneas. For instructions on arrangements and listing of Eye Banks, see Appendix IX.

Bequeathal of Entire Body to a Medical School

Thousands of bodies are needed each year for the training of future doctors and dentists. New medical schools are opening, and the supply of unclaimed bodies is steadily diminishing. Only the rapid increase in the practice of bequeathing bodies has averted a nationwide crisis. Bodies may only be given. They may not be sold. Instructions on how to make arrangements, together with a listing of medical schools, their degree of need and provision for transportation, are given in Appendix IX. Bodies may be donated at death, or after a funeral, with or without viewing, if the funeral director follows the medical school's directions for embalming.

Alternative plans should always be made, as there is no assurance a body will be accepted and the decision is usually made by the medical school at time of death. It helps if the bequeathal form has been filed with the medical shool in advance of death.

Most schools assume responsibility for the final dispostion of the body and will, if requested, return the ashes to the family. This may take as long as two years, but generally can be speeded up if desired.

Bequeathal of Other Organs and Tissues

For more information concerning the need for the following organs and tissues, and organizations concerned with them, see Appendix IX.

These organs and tissues include:

Ear drums and ear bones	Pituitary glands
Kidneys	Skin
Livers	Blood
Hearts	Brain tissue
Pancreas	Artificial implants (for study)
Lungs	

Permission for Autopsy

Another service the dead and their families can render includes permission for autopsy. Such permission should routinely be granted *except* when the body or a major organ is to be donated. Autopsy is often very helpful in improving the knowledge and experience of doctors and in some cases is more valuable than bequeathal. Sometimes it directly benefits the family. Temporal bones, pituitary and sometimes corneas, skin and bone can be retrieved after an autopsy.

Glasses

Glasses left by the dead (or no longer needed by the living) can be sent to New Eyes for the Needy. They have helped over two million people since their founding in 1932.

How to Donate Tissues or Organs

There are several ways:
1. For donating the entire body, see Appendix IX.
2. Check the space provided on the driver's license in most states and provinces.
3. Carry a Uniform Donor Card signed by yourself and two witnesses. This constitutes legal authority for donation under the Canadian Human Tissue Gift Acts and the Anatomical Gift Acts in the U.S. *Be sure a twenty-four-hour number to call is provided* and carry the card with your driver's license, where it will readily be found in case of accident. See Appendix IX for illustration and sources for donor cards.
4. Register with the Living Bank and carry their donor card with twenty-four-hour, toll-free number. The Living Bank has over 120,000 members, as of October 1983, and is growing rapidly. At time of death, they may be called and will immediately contact the nearest appropriate facilities to arrange for use of all possible body parts or donation to a medical school, as desired by the donor. They coordinate with all transplant facilities and organ banks in North America. They receive no tax support and depend entirely on voluntary contributions. We suggest a contribution if you send for their material.
5. Discuss your wishes with your family and doctor. Doctors will not remove an organ without the consent of the family at time of death, even if a donor card has been filled out.
6. Be sure your desire to be an organ donor is entered on your hospital chart. This will help insure that necessary decisions are made without delay.
7. Persons with allergies or other special medical conditions are well advised to register with Medic Alert (see Appendix IX) and wear the tag or bracelet they provide. Should you land unconscious in a hospital, Medic Alert can be called collect and will quickly give the necessary information, including your anatomical gift wishes.

8. Contact Organ Donors Canada for additional information on organ donation in Canada. (See Appendix IX for address.)

Problems of Organ Donation and Possible Solutions

A Serious Shortage: The new successes of transplant therapy have dramatically increased the shortage of organs for transplant. Daily, people die whose lives might be saved if a liver, kidney or heart were available for transplant. Sight and hearing could be restored to thousands if sufficient corneas and ear structures were donated.

Turn Support into Action: Opinion polls show as many as seventy-eight percent of adults ready to serve as organ donors.[3] Yet only one in six has told family members of his/her feelings, and one in ten actually filled out a donor card.[4] The Kidney Foundations are campaigning to turn this silent support into action.

Clarify Definition of Death: Among the many tough questions facing those involved in organ transplantation is how to decide when the death of the donor has occurred. Traditionally, death was defined as the prolonged absence of heartbeat or breathing. Now, machinery may keep heart and lungs functioning long after brain death has occurred—indeed, must do so to preserve the needed organs. Many on both sides of the border support the Canadian Law Reform Commission recommendation that the law specify that "a person is dead when an irreversible cessation of all that person's brain functions has occurred."[5] This would remove one serious hurdle for those with the difficult job of arranging for organ donations at the time of death.

Training Emergency Personnel: It is important that emergency medical and highway patrol personnel be alerted to check for donor cards and information on driver's licenses when identifying traffic victims. Of the estimated 50,000 people who died in motor accidents last year, very few donated organs or tissues, though most were potential donors.

Hospital Records: Routine questions asked of all patients admitted to hospitals should include their wishes concerning organ donation—not a cheerful question to ask perhaps, but relatively easy as a routine formality.

Better Coordination Needed: Efforts are increasing to coordinate donations so that gifts will not be overlooked or wasted. Now, fewer than 30% of hospitals equipped to recover organs do so, and 95% of organs and tissues used are obtained from less than 10% of hospitals.[6] Senators Albert Gore (D-Tenn.) and Ted Kennedy (D-Mass.) have introduced legislation to establish a national registry for organ donation. Transplant coordinators now are employed in most North American transplant centers and work with hospital staffs to encourage and fully utilize organ donations.

Regional tissue banks are encouraged by the American Association of Tissue Banks. A good example of a regional bank is the Northern California Transplant Bank, which handles procurement, processing, storage and distribution of a wide variety of organs and tissues.

Commercial Sale of Organs? An International Kidney Exchange has been proposed to deal in imported kidneys. A price of $10,000 has been suggested, and up to $25,000 has been asked for sale of a kidney.[7] Most people involved with organ donations deplore the idea or selling organs. The legislation proposed by Senator Gore would prohibit such sales.

Heavy Expense: A related problem is the high cost of some transplant surgery. Although organs are donated without charge, medical expenses still range from a minimum of $2,500 for a cornea transplant through an average of $35,000 for a kidney replacement and up to $238,000 for a liver.[8] In Canada, medical costs usually are borne by the government health insurance program. Related expenses, such as travel for family, may not be covered. In the United States, Medicare and Medicaid as well as private insurance companies consider most transplantation experimental and do not cover costs. Medicare pays part of the cost of kidney transplants, and at least one Blue Cross/Blue Shield plan includes transplantation coverage. Private resources usually are required and sometimes are gathered through special fund-raising efforts. Even so, a transplant may be cheaper than long-term hospital care or keeping a person on a kidney dialysis machine.

Universal Donor Legislation: The only complete, long-range solution to the shortage of organs and tissues for therapy and transplant is the Universal Donor Principle, whereby anyone who dies anywhere is available as a donor of needed organs *unless* he or she has specified to the contrary on a "non-donor" card or the family specifies to the contrary. This arrangement is already in effect in France, Greece, Spain, Switzerland, Norway, Sweden and Denmark, and as far as we know, it is working well. Arthur Caplan, of the Hastings Center, vigorously advocates passage of similar legislation in North America.[9]

The Gift of Life: Such legislation and such a practice could save thousands of lives, cure a vast amount of blindness and relieve much suffering. Consider what it might mean. *You* need an organ transplant to save your life. You get one at once. *Your wife* needs a corneal transplant to restore her sight. She gets one immediately. *Your child* is stunted and needs growth hormones. He gets all he needs. Shortages of organs and tissues would be virtually ended. This gives a new and creative dimension to death.

REFERENCES

[1] Quoted in *The Bank Account*, 3:1 (Spring 1982), Published quarterly by The Living Bank. Reprinted by permission of The Living Bank.

[2] "The New Era of Transplants," *Newsweek*, August 19, 1983, pp. 38-44.

[3] Cleveland, SE, "Changes in Human Tissue Donor Attitudes: 1969-1974," *Psychosom. Med.* 37:306-312 (1975).

[4] "Attitudes and Opinions of the American Public Toward Kidney Donations," unpublished report of the Gallup Organization, February 1983.

[5] *Criteria for the Determination of Death,* Law Reform Commission of Canada, 130 Albert St., Ottawa, Ontario, Canada K1A 0L6.

[6] Arthur Caplan, "Cash Market Is No Place for Trade in Vital Organs," *L.A. Times*, Sept. 21, 1983, and "Tip the Balance in Favor of Donations,"*U.S.A. Today,* May 9, 1983.

[7] Arthur Caplan, "Don't Tempt Poor to Risk Their Health," *U.S.A. Today,* Sept. 27, 1983 and "Cash Market," *op. cit.*

[8] *Newsweek*, op. cit.

[9] Arthur Caplan, "Don't Tempt Poor ...," *op. cit.*

Many years ago, when we were discussing a man who was being kept alive artificially after any prospect of a useful or satisfying life was past, my mother remarked, "If you let that happen to me, I'll come back and haunt you!"

When, at age 95, she was in a nursing home, bedridden, almost blind and deaf, and unable to speak coherently, my father came to visit her each afternoon, and to give her supper. There was much warmth and tenderness between them, and this continued to give meaning to her life.

At length as her condition deteriorated she decided that she had gone far enough. Her only recourse was to decline food. The nursing home responded with force-feeding—a brutal process. My father protested. "Offer her food," he said. "Give her every consideration, but do *not* force her!" When they ignored his wishes, he brought them a copy of an article which Mother had written years before, arguing that a person should be free to end his/her own life when his/her physical condition becomes hopeless.* Still they persisted, so my father and brother and I jointly called the doctor, saying, "Get the feeding stopped or get her out of there!" This time they stopped and a few days later Mother died in peace.

I took the death certificate to the county health office while my brother fetched a box from the Friends Burial Committee. When we arrived to claim the body the woman in charge exclaimed she had never heard of such a thing! She had called a funeral director who arrived the same time we did. An unusual confrontation. The funeral director graciously turned to the woman in charge and said, "They know what they're doing," then bowed himself out.

We lifted Mother's body into the box and I took it home in my station wagon. In the morning my daughter-in-law and I took her body to the medical school as she had requested. Mother had been firm about this. She was a biologist and thrifty, too. She had said she "didn't want her body wasted." The medical school would have paid for transportation but this was something I could do for her, a meaningful privilege. At the medical school we lifted Mother's body out of the box which we took back for future use.

That afternoon my niece was being married in a nearby city. We all went. The ceremony was of a Quaker type in which there is no presiding minister, the speaking being done by the principals, and by others who felt moved to speak. This ceremony became a joint celebration of my mother's life and her granddaughter's marriage and was a deeply moving occasion. My father spoke of the "almost unbearable joy" which he felt in the sense of continuity. The next evening we held a Memorial Meeting in the community where Mother had spent most of her life. Family and friends shared their thoughts and memories and extended fellowship and support to one another. That too was a memorable occasion which helped to deepen the quality of our lives.

*"On Drinking the Hemlock," by Lucy G. Morgan. Written in 1927, it was printed in the Dec. 1971 issue of *The Hastings Center Report*. (See Hastings Center, p. 96.)

Appendix I / BIBLIOGRAPHY

General: Books and Pamphlets

Charmaz, Kathy, *The Social Reality of Death: Death in Contemporary America*. Reading, MA: Addison-Wesley Publishing Company, 1980. A clear and comprehensive textbook covering varied approaches to death, dying, ethics, death in medical settings, "extraordinary death," suicide, the funeral industry, and grief and mourning. College and graduate level. Highly recommended.

Conover, Charlotte Reeve, *Harvest of the Years*. Burnsville, NC: Celo Press. This classic on aging is a collection of essays by a woman in her eighties. Written with courage and wisdom, it describes the limitations of age with a touch of humor and points the way to rise above them.

DeSpelder, Lynne Ann, and Albert Lee Strickland, *The Last Dance: Encountering Death and Dying*. Palo Alto, CA: Mayfield Publishing Co., 1983. 491pp. $16.95. Attitudes toward death; cross-cultural and historical perspectives; how children learn about death; health care systems; facing death-cancer; funerals and body disposition; survivors; death in children's lives; medical ethics in a technological age; law and death; risk taking, accidents, disasters, violence, war; suicide; beyond death; personal and social choices. Excellent college text.

Feifel, Herman, *New Meanings of Death*. New York: McGraw Hill, 1977. Outstanding anthology, including Kastenbaum on death and development through the life cycle; Bluebond-Langner on meanings of death to children; Schneidman on death and the college student; Weisman on the psychiatrist and the inexorable; Garfield on the personal impact of death on the clinician; Saunders on St. Christopher's Hospice; Kelly on Make Today Count; Kalish on death and the family; Leviton on death education; Lifton on immortality; Simpson on death and poetry; Gutman on death and power; Shaffer and Rodes on death and the law.

Grollman, Earl A. (ed.), *Concerning Death: A Practical Guide for the Living*. Boston: Beacon Press, 1974. Chapters on Protestant, Catholic and Jewish theology and rituals of death and after life; children and death; final arrangements; bereavement; suicide; and condolence calls and letters. Bibliography.

Irish, Donald P., and Betty Green, *Death Education, Preparation for Living*. Cambridge, MA: Schenkman Publishing Company, 1971. Talks from a symposium on social and personal meanings of death and many aspects of death education.

Irish, Donald P., *Awareness of Death: Preparation for Living.* Religious Education Committee, Friends General Conference, 1502B Race St., Philadelphia, PA 19102, 1976. 28pp. $1.50.

Kastenbaum, Robert J., *Death, Society and Human Experience.* 2nd ed. St. Louis: CV Mosby Co., 1981. 316pp. Paper $13.95. Death happens; death is; death is like; death means; the individual in the death system; disaster and the death system; intimations of mortality (childhood); death as life's companion (adult years); dying, reflection on life; dying, hospice; bereavement, grief; suicide; do we survive death?; death will be. More reflective than "pure" psychology; excellent anthology.

Knott, J.E., Mary C. Ribar, Betty Duxon and Marc King, *Thanatopics: A Manual of Structured Learning Experiences for Death Education.* SLE Publications, P.O. Box 52, Kingston, RI 01881, 1982. $12.20 plus $1.50 shipping. Fifty exercises for use in death education classes.

Kubler-Ross, Elisabeth, *On Children and Death.* New York: Macmillan Publishing Co., 1983. 279pp. $12.95. Practical and compassionate discussion of physical, emotional and spiritual aspects of the death of a child from the point of view of the child, siblings and parents.

Kubler-Ross, Elisabeth, *Death: The Final Stage of Growth.* Englewood Cliffs, NJ: Prentice-Hall, Inc., 1975. Essays on the philosophies of death and after life of Hinduism and Buddhism, practices of Judaism and Alaskan Indians; attitudes of hospital personnel and personal experiences of death as a growthful experience from the perspective of both the dying and the bereaved.

Kubler-Ross, Elisabeth, *On Death and Dying: What the Dying Have to Teach Doctors, Nurses, Clergy and Their Own Families.* New York: Macmillan Publishing Co., 1969. Based on counseling dying hospital patients, this book describes Kubler-Ross' five stages of dying and brings to public attention the need of the dying to be treated as fully alive and human.

Lifton, Robert Jay, *The Broken Connection.* New York: Simon and Schuster, 1979. Extended critique of Freudian theories relating to death and immortality, and Lifton's analysis of the effects of awareness of death, including the survivor experience and the pursuit of immortality; analysis of the impact of modern holocaust experiences and the rise of "nuclearism."

Lifton, Robert Jay, *Home from the War: Vietnam Veterans: Neither Victims nor Executioners.* New York: Simon and Schuster, 1974. Describes Lifton's experiences as counselor in Vietnam Veterans' support groups, and how they coped with "death immersion." Personal, vivid, readable.

Norwich Peace Center, "Freeze It!", Box 283, Norwich, VT 05055. 32-page pamphlet, $.50. Concise and carefully documented report on the arms race and ways to control it.

Schneidman, Edwin S., *Death: Current Perspectives,* 3rd ed. Palo Alto, CA: Mayfield Publishing Co., 1980, paper $15.95. Concepts of death; death as a social disease; demography of death; determination of death; participants of death; survivors of death; psychological aspects; death and dignity; life after death?; self-destructions; poetic epilogue; annotated bibliography. Highly recommended.

Simpson, Michael A., *Dying, Death and Grief: A Critically Annotated Bibliography and Source Book of Thanatology and Terminal Care.* New York and London: Plenum Press, 1979. Describes and rates over 700 books. Highly recommended.

Wass, Hannelore, Charles A. Corr, Richard A. Pacholski, and Catherine M. Sanders, *Death Education: An Annotated Resource Guide.* New York: Hemisphere Publishing Corporation, 1980, 303pp., $27.90. Over 1,000 listings of printed materials, audiovisual resources, organizations, and community resources.

General: Periodicals

Canadian Journal on Aging (formerly *Essence*), published by Canadian Association on Gerontology, Stephen Fleming, Managing Editor, Atkinson College, York University, Downsview, Ontario, Canada.

Death Education: Pedagogy, Counseling, Care—an International Quarterly, edited by Hannelore Wass, College of Education, University of Florida, Gainesville, FL 32611. International, interdisciplinary, professional sharing of experience, techniques, ideas for teaching and counseling.

New Advances in Thanatology (formerly *Journal of Thanatology*), published by Foundation of Thanatology, 630 West 168th St., New York, NY 10032.

Hastings Center Report, Hastings-on-Hudson: Institute of Society, Ethics, and the Life Sciences, The Hastings Center. Bimonthly. Articles pertinent to ethical issues of death and dying.

Omega: Journal of Death and Dying, edited by Robert Kastenbaum, College 1, University of Mass., Columbia Point Campus, Dorchester, MA 02125.

General: Audiovisuals

National Information Center for Educational Media, University of Southern California, Los Angeles, provides listings, alphabetically and under subject headings, annotated for content, audience level and availability, for educational audio tapes, educational videotapes, 16mm educational films and 35mm educational filmstrips.

Wass, Hannelore, et al., *Death Education: An Annotated Resource Guide,* see "Books and Pamphlets."

Living with Dying (See also General listings)

Cohen, Kenneth P., Ph.D., *Hospice: Prescription for Terminal Care.* Germantown, MD: Aspen Systems Corporation, 1979, $34.00. Comprehensive text on history, theory and practice of hospice.

Davidson, Glen, ed., *The Hospice: Development and Administration.* Washington: Hemisphere Publishing Corporation, 1978. Has the depth and scope required by the health professions.

Duda, Deborah, *A Guide to Dying at Home.* John Muir Publications, P.O. Box 613, Santa Fe, NM 87501, 1982, $7.50 plus $1.25 postage. Practical and comprehensive handbook on home care. Highly recommended.

Glaser, Barney and Anselm Strauss, *Awareness of Dying.* Chicago: Aldine Publishing, 1964. Classic sociological description of styles and levels of awareness and communication about impending death by patients, families and staff in a hospital setting.

Gold, Margaret, Ph.D., *Life Support: What Families Say About Hospital, Hospice and Home Care for the Fatally Ill.* Mount Vernon, NY: Consumers Union Foundation, 1983. Study based on interviews with 40 primary caregiver/close relatives of people who were cared for at home (88%) or in nursing facility in last year of life. Very revealing of caregiver feelings about good and bad aspects of their situations.

Hamilton, Michael P., and Helen F. Reid, *Hospice Handbook.* Grand Rapids: William B. Eerdmans Publishing Co., 1980, 196pp., paper, $5.95.

Jury, Mark and Dan, *Gramp.* New York: Grossman Publishers (Viking Press), 1976, paper. A moving and honest account of the death at home of an 82-year-old senile man, reported in word and photograph by his family, who honored his wishes and cared for him with love.

Kelly, Orville E., *Until Tomorrow Comes.* New York: Everest House, 1979. Canada: Beaverbooks. Final book by the founder of Make Today Count organization, synthesizing and expanding earlier writing about facts of cancer, patient and family reactions, and how to live with cancer. Good for patients, families and care givers.

Lund, Dores, *Eric.* New York: Dell Publishing Co., 1974, 267pp. paper $1.75. Story of Eric's struggle against leukemia as a young college man, told by his mother.

Martinson, I.M., *Home Care for the Dying Child.* New York: Appleton-Century/Croft, 1976.

National Hospice Organization, *Hospice Audio-Visuals: A Resource Guide.* 1901 N. Fort Myer Dr., Arlington, VA 22209. Catalog of more than 100 productions, screened by Film Review Committee of the 1983 NHO Annual Meeting. $5 plus $1 postage.

Stoddard, Sandol, *The Hospice Movement: A Better Way of Caring for the Dying.* New York: Vintage Books (paperback). A clear and inexpensive exposition for the layman. Recommended.

Bereavement (See also General listings)

Arnold, Joan Hagan and Penelope Buschman Gemma, *A Child Dies: A Portrait of Family Grief.* Rockville, MD: Aspen Systems Corporation, 1983. Sensitive discussions of the meaning a child's death has for parents, the process of mourning and how these vary with the age of the child who dies.

Family Living Series, *Newborn Death.* Centering Corporation, P.O. Box 3367, Omaha, NE 68103-0367, 26pp. $2.35. For parents, encouraging them to take an active part in decision-making and in seeing, holding, touching and naming their baby who has died; recognizes the couple's grief, residual effects, and the importance of marriage and other close relationships. See Centering Corporation in Appendix II for additional resources.

Grollman, Earl A., *Talking About Death: A Dialogue Between Parent and Child.* Boston: Beacon Press, 1971. Models a direct and sensitive way of discussing a death in the family, exploring the child's feelings and reassuring him or her.

Head, Joseph and S.L. Cranson (eds.), *Reincarnation: The Phoenix Fire Mystery.* New York: Julian Press/Crown Publishers, Inc.; Warner Books, paper. Comprehensive discussion of major viewpoints about reincarnation.

Jensen, Amy Hillyard, *Healing Grief.* Medic Publishing Co., P.O. Box 89, Redmond, WA 98052, 22pp., $1.25 postpaid; low bulk rates. The most concise, comprehensive and helpful information for bereaved parents that we found.

Kohn, William K. and Jane Burgess Kohn, *Widower.* Bacon Press, 1978. A widower relates his personal experiences, including comment based on interviews with many other widowers.

LeShan, Eda, *Learning to Say Goodby.* New York: Macmillan, 1976. Also Avon paperback. A loving, sensitive book for children ages 9-10.

Lichtman, Wendy, *Blew and the Death of the Mag.* Freestone Publishing Co., Box 357, Albion, CA 95410, 1975. A prose-poem for children ages 8-12 describing a child's process of grief and healing for the death of a friend.

Moody, Raymond, *Life After Life.* Mockingbird. Interviews with persons revived after near death. Introduction by Elisabeth Kubler-Ross.

Pincus, Lily, *Death and the Family: The Importance of Mourning.* New York: Pantheon Books, 1974. Vintage, paper. Social worker writes from extensive counseling experience about family crises and adjustments created by death. Especially good on widowhood.

Raphael, Beverly, *The Anatomy of Grief.* New York: Basic Books, 1983, 405pp. plus references, $27.50. Examines, evaluates and integrates the literature; follows a lifespan perspective; ends with chapters on disasters and caring for the bereaved. Scholarly, comprehensive. Highly recommended.

Riemer, Jack, *Jewish Reflections on Death.* New York: Schocken Books, 1974. An anthology reflecting the psychological and spiritual wisdom of Jewish law and tradition concerning death and mourning. Explores modern problems relating to death, from the Jewish experience of suffering and solace. Valuable as well to non-Jews.

Ring, Kenneth, *Life at Death: A Scientific Investigation of the Near Death Experience.* New York: Coward, McCann and Geoghegan, 1980. $11.95. Examines alternative explanations of these experiences.

Schatz, William H., *Healing a Father's Grief.* Medic Publishing Co., P.O. Box 89, Redmond WA 98052, 1984. 24pp., $1.25 postpaid, low bulk rates. For bereaved fathers; direct and practical; highly recommended.

Schoenberg, Bernard, Arthur C. Carr, David Peretz, Austin Kutscher and Evan K. Goldberg (eds.), *Anticipatory Grief.* New York: Columbia University Press, 1974. Comprehensive, readable articles grouped under the titles: Introductory Concepts, Clinical Aspects, Childhood Illness, The Health Professions, The Management of Anticipatory Grief, and Pastoral Aspects. Recommended.

Schoenberg, Bernard, Arthur C. Carr, David Peretz, Austin Kutscher (eds.), *Loss and Grief: Psychological Management in Medical Practice.* New York: Columbia University Press, 1970. Classic, comprehensive and readable; takes a broad perspective.

Vail, Elaine, *A Personal Guide to Living with Loss.* John Wiley & Sons, Inc., 1982. Discusses euthanasia, suicide, near-death experiences, cryonics, definitions of death.

Wass, Hannelore, and Charles A. Corr, *Helping Children Cope with Death: Guidelines and Resources.* Washington: Hemisphere Publishing Corporation, 1982. Includes 75 pages of bibliography with 140 annotated audiovisual listings.

Watson, Elizabeth, *Guests of My Life.* Burnsville, NC: Celo Press, 1979. Moving personal account of a mother's journey through grief for the loss of her grown daughter; describes the insight and comfort received from works of Tagore, Whitman, Dickinson, Mansfield, Paton and Rilke. $6.95, paper.

Westberg, Granger E., *Good Grief: A Constructive Approach to the Problem of Loss.* Philadelphia: Fortress Press, 1962 and 1971. Available in regular or large print. For the layman, brief and clear descriptions of the phases of grief; religious viewpoint, for all faiths.

Right to Die

Alvarez, A., *The Savage God.* New York: Bantam, paper. Historical, literary and philosophical review of suicide, including descriptions of Alvarez's friendship with Sylvia Plath and his own suicide attempt.

Brodie, Howard, *Ethical Decisions in Medicine.* Boston: Little, Brown & Co., 1976. Examines issues of informed consent, quality of life, ethical participation, allocation of scarce resources, and euthanasia. Highly recommended for anyone involved in this area.

Hewett, John, *After Suicide.* Philadelphia: Westminster Press, 1980.

Humphrey, Derek, *Let Me Die before I Wake: Hemlock's Book of Self-Deliverance for the Dying.* The Hemlock Society, P.O. Box 66218, Los Angeles, CA 90066, 1981. $10. Case stories of assisted suicides by terminally ill persons; compassionate discussion of emotional, legal and physical aspects of self-deliverance. Good bibliography.

Klagsbrun, Francine, *Too Young to Die: Youth and Suicide.* rev. ed. New York: Pocket Books, 1981, paper, $2.50. Most youthful suicides could be prevented by learning the danger signals and knowing what to do.

Law Reform Commission of Canada, *Euthanasia, Aiding Suicide and Cessation of Treatment.* 1982. Available by mail, free, from the Commission at 130 Albert St., 7th Floor, Ottawa, K1A 0L6, Canada.

Maguire, Daniel C., *Death by Choice.* New York: Schocken Books, 1974. 224pp., paper. Marquette University theologian wrestles with ethical questions of death by choice: deciding for yourself; deciding for others; legal killing (abortion, capital punishment, suicide, euthanasia, war). Highly recommended.

Plath, Sylvia, *The Bell Jar.* New York: Bantam paperback. Autobiographical novel about a 19-year-old girl who attempts suicide. Offers excellent insight into suicidal thinking.

Robertson, John A., *The Rights of the Critically Ill.* ACLU Handbook, Bantam Books, 1983.

Suicide and Life-threatening Behavior. Quarterly journal, 11431 Kingsland St., Los Angeles CA 90066.

Simple Burial (See also Appendix VII—CAFMS Publications.)

Bowman, LeRoy, *The American Funeral.* Westport, CT: Greenwood Press, reprinted 1973. Classic sociological study.

Consumers Union, *Funerals: Consumers' Last Rights.* Mount Vernon, NY 10550, 1977. Detailed and comprehensive discussion of consumer options in funeral arrangements, including body donations, memorial societies, pre-need planning, relevant laws, autopsy, organ transplant, and respective costs.

Mitford, Jessica, *The American Way of Death.* 1979, Fawcett, paper $2.95.

Nelson, Thomas C., *It's Your Choice: The Practical Guide to Planning a Funeral.* "A Consumer Action Project of American Association of Retired Persons," Glenview, IL: Scott, Foresman and Company, 1983. $4.95 plus $1.30 shipping and handling from AARP Books, 400 S. Edward St., Mount Prospect, IL 60056.

Porter, Sylvia, *Sylvia Porter's Money Book: How to Earn It, Spend It, Save It, Invest It, Borrow It— and Use It to Better Your Life.* Garden City, NY: Doubleday & Company, Inc., 1975. Thorough, practical advice by a leading financial columnist. Available in paperback.

Appendix II / ORGANIZATIONS

American Association of Suicidology, Dept. of Health, 2151 Berkeley Way, Berkeley, CA 94704.

American Cancer Society, 777 Third Ave., New York, NY 10017. Through regional and local groups provides sick room equipment for home use, reference material for doctors, support services. National program of research and education.

Candlelighters Foundation, 2025 Eye St., N.W., Suite 1011, Washington, DC 20006. Support groups for families of children with cancer; 155 member groups in 1983. Newsletter.

Center for Information on Suicide, 6377 Lake Apopka Place, San Diego, CA 92119. Provides directory of books, cassettes, articles.

Centering Corporation, P.O. Box 3367, Omaha, NE 68103-0367, founded 1977, non-profit, tax-exempt, provides workshops, newsletter, filmstrips, and booklets on patient education for children, and for siblings and parents bereaved through miscarriage, newborn death, death of older children or grandparents. Highly recommended.

The Compassionate Friends, P.O. Box 1347, Oak Brook, IL 60521. Support groups for bereaved parents. 315 local groups in 1983. Quarterly newsletter.

Concern for Dying, 250 West 57th St., New York, NY 10107, (formerly Euthanasia Educational Fund). Distributes Living Will, newsletters, and other educational materials supporting the right to die, sponsors conferences and workshops.

Connecticut Hospice Institute for Education, Training and Research, 61 Burban Drive, Branford, CT 06405. "To weave the hospice concept and philosophy into the fabric of the health-care system; to enhance the skills and awareness of caregivers working with terminally ill patients and families." Continuing education courses for professionals and volunteer administrators. Produces films and video tapes.

Continental Association of Funeral and Memorial Societies (see Appendix VII).

Forum for Death Education and Counseling, 2211 Arthur Ave., Lakewood, OH 44107. Non-profit association of death education teachers and counselors in U.S. and Canada. $35/year membership includes monthly newsletter, discounts on *Death Education* and *Canadian Journal on Aging.* Annual conference.

Foundation of Thanatology, 630 W 168th St., New York, NY 10032. Extensive library, symposia on psychological aspects of dying, reactions to death, loss and grief. Scientific and theoretical emphasis.

Grief Education Institute, 2422 S. Downing St., Denver, CO 80210. Founded by bereaved parents, provides information on grief and bereavement, particularly for parents and families.

The Hastings Center: Institute of Society, Ethics and the Life Sciences, 360 Broadway, Hastings-on-Hudson, NY 10706. Publishes bi-monthly *Hastings Center Report,* articles, book reviews, and annual annotated bibliographies, and holds conferences on bio-medical ethics, including issues relating to death and dying.

Hemlock Society. P.O. Box 66218, Los Angeles, CA 90066. Provides information and support for voluntary euthanasia (self-deliverance) for terminally ill adults and also for the seriously, incurably physically ill.

Hospice of Marin, 77 Mark Drive #17, San Rafael, CA 94903. Local hospice with strong national outreach for information and training.

International Council for Infant Survival, P.O. Box 3841, Davenport, IA 52808. Founded by and for parents of SIDS victims; 93 local groups in 1983. (Formerly Guild for Infant Survival.)

Loving Outreach for Survivors of Sudden-Death [L.O.S.S.]. P.O. Box 7303, Stn. M, Edmonton, Alberta T5E 6C8, Canada. Newly formed support group; send $2 and indicate cause of death to receive packet of very helpful information for survivors.

Make Today Count, P.O. Box 303, Burlington, IA 52601. Mutual support organization of persons with life-threatening illness and their families, to "help each other live in a positive, meaningful manner." Over 250 local chapters in 1984, worldwide.

Mended Hearts, 721 Huntington Ave., Boston, MA 02115. Support groups of people who have had open-heart surgery. Periodicals. 75 local groups in 1980.

Minnesota Center for Pregnancy Loss, 1465 E. Wayzata Blvd., Suite 22, Minneapolis, MN 55351. Support, referrals and education after miscarriage, stillbirth and newborn death.

Minnesota Coalition for Terminal Care, 1901 University Ave., S.E., Minneapolis, MN 55414. Bibliographies, speakers, information on educational resources. Newsletter, $12 a year.

National Association for Widowed People, P.O. Box 3564, Springfield, IL 62708. 3,000 local groups, newsletter and quarterly periodical.

National Funeral Directors Association, 135 Wells St., Milwaukee, WI 53202. Leading trade association in the funeral industry. Provides literature, audiovisual materials and speakers on many aspects of bereavement and funeral planning.

National Hospice Organization (see Appendix IV).

National Self-Help Clearinghouse, Graduate School and University Center, City University of New York, 33 West 42nd St., Room 1206-A, New York, NY 10036. Provides information on peer support groups of all kinds.

National SIDS Foundation, 2 Metro Plaza, 8240 Professional Place, Landover, MD 20785. 70 local groups, newsletter.

Parents of Murdered Children, 1739 Bella Vista, Cincinnati, OH 45237. Founded by parent survivors in 1978, for parents and other survivors of murder victims. Provides information, advocacy and newsletter to meet the unique needs of murder survivors. Local support groups.

St. Francis Center, 1768 Church St., N.W., Washington, DC 20036. A nonprofit, non-sectarian organization providing counseling for persons facing a life-threatening illness and/or bereavement, conducts educational and training programs in the area of death and dying, offers practical and emotional assistance with dignified low cost funerals, and supplies pine coffins, coffin plans and ash boxes. Brochures available on request.

Seasons: Suicide Bereavement, 4777 Naniloa Drive, Salt Lake City, UT 84117. Support group for "survivor-victims" of suicide. National group with local chapters forming.

Shanti Nilaya, P.O. Box 2396, Escondido, CA 92025. Healing and growth center founded by Elisabeth Kubler-Ross;

educational and inspirational materials, newsletter, counseling and workshops for the dying and their families, the bereaved, the handicapped (in coming to terms with their "little deaths"), and those working with them.

Society for the Right to Die. 250 West 57th St., New York, NY 10107, distributes the "Living Will," lobbies for Natural Death Act Laws. (Formerly Euthanasia Society of America.)

Suicide Prevention Center, Inc., 184 Salem Ave., Dayton, OH 45406, provides pamphlets, manuals, audio-visuals.

THEOS Foundation, 306 Penn Hills Mall, Pittsburgh, PA 15235. Self-help groups for widowed women, church affiliated. Monthly newsletter.

Widowed Persons Service. National Retired Teachers Association and American Association of Retired Persons, 1909 K Street, N.W., Washington, DC 20049 (eastern office); Box 199, Long Beach, CA 90801 (western office). Provides assistance in developing local support programs for widowed people, public education about needs of the widowed and services available, directory of services for widowed persons. Free pamphlet "On Being Alone."

Appendix III / SUGGESTIONS FOR TEACHERS

General

A broad range of ideas, attitudes and practices relating to death throughout history and among various cultures may be explored through works of history, literature, anthropology, sociology, religion and philosophy. In discussing these readings and ideas, students will begin to feel at ease with the language of death. Moving gradually from general ideas to their own experiences, students will become comfortable with topics which may be difficult.

Useful literary works include Tolstoy's *Death of Ivan Illych*, Camus' *The Stranger*, Agee's *Death in the Family*, Edward Albee's play "The Sandbox," Thornton Wilder's "Our Town," Arthur Miller's "Death of a Salesman," the poetry of Sylvia Plath, Emily Dickinson, John Donne and Kahlil Gibran, and Biblical accounts of the death of Jesus. Additional books are listed in the bibliography. See particularly *Thanatopics*, by J.E. Knott, *Death Education*, by Hannelore Wass, and the National Information Center for Educational Media.

Questions for Class Discussion: It is sometimes said that the quality of a life is more important than its length. What do we mean by the quality of a life?

What if death really took a holiday and no one died? What would happen? Would you really want to live forever? Would you like to have your body deep frozen when you died if you thought you might be restored to life in some future time? (People actually do this.)

What time of life is best? Childhood? Young adulthood? Middle age? Old age? Children in our culture are given the impression that youth is the favored time of life. Is this sound?

Life is interdependent. How does humankind fit into this interdependency? An estimated 1,200 species have become extinct in the past 75 years (mainly as a result of human activity). How does the death of a species differ from the death of an individual?

Role Playing: Role playing is useful for developing ideas and understanding and for enabling students to talk about death. One group method is to call for volunteers (or assign roles) and have the role playing done by a single team, while the rest of the group observes. When the role playing is finished, those playing the roles give their reactions first, then the rest of the group. An excellent variation (or sequel) is to divide the group into subgroups containing, in addition to the role players, one or more observers. When a role play has been completed, the observer comments on it and gives his or her own reactions. The subgroups then reassemble in the complete group where each observer reports and general discussion follows.

Role playing topics need not be related to the ages and circumstances of the players though it is more interesting if they are. Care should be taken, in any role-playing exercise, to avoid pressuring anyone to take part, either as a participant or observer.

Suggestions for Role Playing: Patient *A* asks Doctor *B* what the prospects are. The doctor knows that the odds are perhaps ten to one against recovery. How will the doctor phrase his reply and give moral support to the patient?

* * * * *

A, who is in good health, has decided what death arrangements he would like and also what type of services. *A* must now explain his wishes to *B*, a close relative whose understanding and cooperation are desired.

A variation of this is for *A* to be on his deathbed.

* * * * *

A dying patient, *A*, wishes to talk about death, but none of the family are willing or able to do it. Accordingly, *A* has asked *B* (friend) to visit so they can have a discussion.

* * * * *

Parent *A* is comforting child *B* on the death of a pet. How can this be made a positive and maturing experience?

* * * * *

A was thought to be dying of cancer and had accepted the situation. Then, through chemotherapy or spontaneous remission the patient is apparently recovering. *A* is talking with another family member, *B*, about what she hopes to do in this "post morten" life, how the world looks, and how things are going to be different.

Self-Written Epitaphs: When students have become somewhat familiar with discussing death, they may be asked to write epitaphs for themselves. (The instructor should do it, too!) This can be an assignment to be presented at the next session. These self-written epitaphs commonly reveal a person's values or image of him or herself. Invite students to read their epitaphs but don't require it. Have the class members fill out their own death certificates; also to write their own obituaries—maybe two obituaries, one as it would be now and another as they would like it to be one, five or even twenty years from now. Students should be invited but *not* required to read these to the group.

Living with Dying

Class discussions may deal with the experience of aging, facing terminal illness, relating to a dying person, hospice and home care.

Questions for Discussion: How does it feel to be told you're dying? How are the terminally ill defined by themselves and others? What is daily life like for the "condemned?" Do people fear death itself, or is it the process of dying, the possibility of a bad afterlife, or concern for the suffering their death may cause others?

Nurses, doctors, social workers, hospice workers or nursing home staff members who work with the dying are good speakers or resource persons to invite to the class.

If circumstances are right and the group is small, a visit with a person who has only a short time to live can be an inspiration to the visitors and a pleasure to the person being visited. Visiting a hospice or nursing home will also stimulate thought and discussion.

Bereavement

Good resource people for class discussions of bereavement include counselors who work with the bereaved, members of a support group for the bereaved, or hospice workers.

Right to Die—Suggested Discussion Topics and Activities

"No man is an island"—only rarely is a person not involved with or responsible to others, persons with whom he or she interacts and who would be affected by his/her death. The potential suicide should consider carefully the effect of his death on others—his parents, his spouse, his friends, his children, his business associates. Is he being selfish?

What does suicide achieve? Does it accomplish what it was intended to do? What is sacrificed—potential accomplishments, pleasures or otherwise—for oneself and for others?

A suicide attempt is often really just a desperate call for help. Sometimes the person is saying, "I'm suffering. I want you to suffer, too." If suicide is a negative reaction to circumstances, what would be some positive reactions?

Make a list of people who failed many times before achieving success or fame. Make a list of people who did not achieve success before reaching the age of fifty.

What other life-denying or life-threatening acts, besides suicide, are common?

The class may visit a hot-line or crisis center and learn how they respond to calls for help. Some members of the class may want to volunteer their services for this.

Simple Burial and Cremation

Questions for Discussion: What kind of arrangements do you prefer? Burial? Cremation? Medical school? Why?

Resource People: A memorial society representative or funeral director can talk to the class. A lawyer or insurance person can discuss wills and estate planning.

Death Ceremonies

Students may be asked to plan a funeral or memorial service for themselves, choosing the type of service and the specific setting, readings, music, or other activities by which they would like others to remember them or express their lives. For some groups these may be actual plans to be placed on record.

It may be of interest to invite a minister, a funeral director and a memorial society representative to meet with the class.

How the Dead Can Help the Living

Questions for Discussion: How does the class feel about having organs or tissues from their bodies used after they die?

Resource People: If there is a medical school or transplant center near, there is probably a transplant coordinator or anatomist who can discuss the need for organs and tissues. Representatives or organizations listed in Appendix IX will probably also be glad to come to discuss the needs and issues involved.

Appendix IV / HOSPICE ORGANIZATIONS

National Hospice Organization, 1901 N. Fort Myer Drive, Suite 402, Arlington, VA 22209. National coordinating body for hospice organizations—sponsors national and regional meetings, develops standards of care, provides educational materials and newsletter, advocates hospice coverage by governmental and private insurance programs.

State Hospice Organizations

ALABAMA: Alabama State Hospice Organization, c/o Joseph Bancroft, MD, 800 Montclair Rd., Birmingham, AL 35213.

ARIZONA: Arizona State Hospice Organization, c/o R. Bradford Walker, Hospice of Tucson, Inc., 5504 East Pima, Tucson, AZ 85712.

ARKANSAS: Arkansas State Hospice Association, P.O. Box 725, Jonesboro, AR 72401.

CALIFORNIA: Northern California Hospice Organization, 703 Market St., San Francisco, CA 94103.

COLORADO: Colorado Hospice Organization, 3534 Kirkwood Pl., Boulder, CO 80302.

CONNECTICUT: Hospice Council of Conn., c/o The VNA of Bridgeport, 1054 North Ave., Bridgeport, CT 06606.

FLORIDA: Hospices of Florida, Inc., c/o Hospice of Boca Raton, 1840 N. Dixie Hwy., Boca Raton, FL 33432.

GEORGIA: Georgia Hospice Organization, c/o Sister Rose McLarney, 2260 Wrightsboro Rd., Augusta, GA 30910.

ILLINOIS: Illinois State Hospice Organization, c/o Illinois Cancer Council, 36 S. Wabash Ave., Suite 700, Chicago, IL 60603.

INDIANA: Indiana Hospice Association, 5002 Tacoma Ave., Ft. Wayne, IN 46807.

IOWA: Iowa Hospice Organization, 205 Loma St., Waterloo, IA 50701.

KANSAS: Association of Kansas Hospices, Hospice of the Plains, 507 Elm, Hays, KS 67601.

KENTUCKY: Kentucky Association of Hospices, 465 E. High St., Lexington, KY 40502.

MAINE: Coalition of Maine Hospices, c/o Cushman Anthony, Hospice of Maine, 32 Thomas Street, Portland, ME 04102.

MARYLAND: Maryland State Hospice Network, c/o Sinai Hospital HC/H, 2401 Belvedere, Baltimore, MD 21215.

MASSACHUSETTS: Hospice Federation of Mass., Inc., c/o Linda Kilburn, Pres., P.O. Box 144, Waban, MA 02168.

MICHIGAN: Michigan Hospice Organization, 1825 Watson Road, Hemlock, MI 48626.

MINNESOTA: Minnesota Hospice Organization, St. John's Hospital Hospice Program, 403 Maria Ave., St. Paul, MN 55106.

MISSOURI: Missouri State Hospice Organization, Adell Peterson, 609 Cherry, #304, Springfield, MO 65801.

MONTANA: Montana Hospice Exchange Council, Bonnie Adee, Coordinator, Hospice of St. Peter's Comm. Hospital, Helena, MT 59601.

NEBRASKA: Nebraska Hospice Association, Susan Salladay, Ph.D., Sec.,

Univ. of Nebraska Med. Center, 42nd and Dewey Ave., Omaha, NE 68105.

NEW HAMPSHIRE: Hospice Affiliates of N.H., Inc., Box 1221, Concord, NH 03301.

NEW JERSEY: New Jersey Hospice Organization, 760 Alexander Rd., CN-1, Princeton, NJ 08340.

NEW YORK: New York State Hospice Association, Inc., 2929 Main St., Buffalo, NY 14214.

NORTH CAROLINA: Hospice of North Carolina, Inc., 800 St. Mary's St., #401, Raleigh, NC 27605.

OHIO: Ohio Hospice Organization, Inc., 2181 Embury Park Rd., Dayton, OH 45414.

OKLAHOMA: Central Oklahoma Hospice Organization, c/o Virginia Staple, R.N., 4500 N. Lincoln Blvd., Oklahoma City, OK 73105.

OREGON: Oregon Council of Hospices, VNA of Portland, P.O. Box 3426, Portland, OR 97203.

PENNSYLVANIA: Pennsylvania Hospice Network, P.O. Box 4634, Pittsburgh, PA 15206.

SOUTH CAROLINA: Hospice of South Carolina, c/o Chaplain William Major,

Pres., Crafts Farrow State Hospital, 7901 Farrow Rd., Columbia, SC 29203.

TENNESSEE: Hospice of Tennessee, 1908 21st Ave. South, Nashville, TN 37212.

TEXAS: Texas Hospice Organization, VAN of Dallas Home Hospice, 2818 Maple Ave., Suite 103, Dallas, TX 75201.

UTAH: Utah Hospice Organization, 1400 N. 500 E, Logan, UT 84321.

VERMONT: Hospice Council of Vermont, RD 2, Box 505, Hinesburg, VT 05461.

VIRGINIA: Virginia State Association of Hospices, c/o Dr. John Mattern, Pres., Riverside Hospital Hospice Program, 500 J. Clyde Morris Blvd., Newport News, VA 23601.

WASHINGTON: Washington State Hospice Organization, 7814 Greenwood Ave. N., Seattle, WA 98103.

WEST VIRGINIA: West Virginia State Hospice Organization, c/o Lawrence Papi, Executive Director, Clara Welty Hospice, Inc., 109 Main St., Wheeling, WV 26003.

WISCONSIN: Hospice Organization of Wisconsin, c/o St. Joseph Hospital, 5000 W. Chambers St., Milwaukee, WI 53210.

Financial Help for Terminal Care

Medicare: This is an insurance program administered by the Social Security System. Coverage is optional for Social Security beneficiaries. This may pay for skilled nursing, some home health aids, medical social worker services; also medical supplies and appliances when prescribed by a doctor and furnished by a home health agency certified by the state government. Usually there is an annual deductible of $75 and co-payment of 20% for expenses above the deductible.

Some 50% of Medicare expenses are incurred by patients in the last year of life. This strongly suggests that many terminal patients are undergoing costly and distressing treatment primarily intended to prolong life, when they should be receiving less costly but more humane hospice care.

Since November 1, 1983, Medicare will pay for services provided by a Medicare-certified hospice program, servicing Medicare-insured persons whose death is anticipated within six months. This may include medicines given at home, custodial care, and counseling. These are covered by a daily rate and do not require separate authorizations for each expense.

However, this will help people mainly in urban areas served by larger hospice organizations, rather than patients in small hospice programs unable to meet the administrative and bookkeeping requirements of the Medicare-Hospice regulations. Although a majority of hospices in North Carolina, for example, will not qualify for Medicare benefits, they will continue to work with other sources of funding.

Medicare coverage of hospice costs will be up for renewal in Congress in September, 1986.

Medicaid: This is a state-supervised, county-administered program whose benefits and requirements vary from state to state. If your income is near the poverty level and you own no more than your house, car and minimal savings, you may be eligible. Ask your county Social Service Department or the equivalent. Medicaid generally has a deductible amount (spend-down), after which it covers 100% of such expenses as medicines, skilled nursing, doctor's visits, medical supplies and appliances. This is especially important for children and younger adults not eligible for Medicare.

Tips on Dealing with Bureaucracies: Always make a note of the date of any conversation, the person you spoke with and the substance of what was said. Keep an orderly file of all written communication. If delays and/or contradictions arise, this will make it much easier to check back on your understanding and resolve the problem. If delay or confusion persists, don't hesitate to ask for a resolution from a supervisor.

Some local and many state governments have telephone numbers which citizens may call to obtain accurate information about government programs. (Sometimes local employees understandably get confused with all the changes in regulations.) Also, you can ask a hospital or health department social worker, or a citizen advocacy group. In most offices there is someone you can talk to as one human being to another. Keep going until you find that person.

Private Insurance: Coverage of hospice expense, formerly rare among insurance companies, is beginning to be accepted as a way of reducing medical costs for terminal care. The National Hospice Organization reported in February 1984 that 13 major health insurance carriers offer, or plan to offer, hospice coverage, though levels of coverage and availability vary greatly among the companies.[1]

Some insurance companies will cover home care services not mentioned in the policy—if you can demonstrate that they will save money by avoiding hospital or nursing home care. Helen Farmer, of the Los Angeles Memorial Society, kept her husband at home during his last weeks but could not leave her job. She explained the situation to the insurance companies and received cooperation in meeting the costs of professional care and equipment. The companies saved money.

It is reasonable to ask one's insurance company, preferably in advance of need, whether and under what conditions their coverage will apply to home care. A hospital chart carefully kept and signed by an M.D. or an R.N. (with the letters after the name) may be helpful.

Legislation has been introduced in Maryland and in Michigan to require private insurance companies to include hospice in their benefits. The National Hospice Organization is actively supporting such legislation.

Other Assistance: Housekeeper or chore services, home health aids and other support services may be available for those eligible. In cities a good place to start is in the Information and Referral Service, usually listed in the Yellow Pages under Social Services. Again hospital, health department and hospice social workers are usually familiar with available services and eligibility.

REFERENCE

[1] *Hospice News,* 2:1, February 1984, "Hospice Insurance Growing in Popularity," p.5.

Appendix V / LIVING WILL

A *Living Will* is a document instructing one's doctor and family to refrain from using extreme measures to prolong the process of dying. A *Durable Power of Attorney* is a document giving someone else the legal authority to determine whether to continue treatment in a terminal illness if the patient is unconscious or incompetent.

Shown below are the states in which a living will has legal status through a Natural Death Act (NDA) and in which a durable power of attorney (DPA) is recognized. Two forms of living wills are given.

Legal recognition is helpful, but in practice a hospital is unlikely to carry out a person's wishes unless they are firmly attested to by the doctor and those family members who have an active concern. It is best, by far, to seek such agreement and get it in writing when death is not in early prospect. To discuss the matter when the family is confronted with an imminent death is much harder but can still be done.

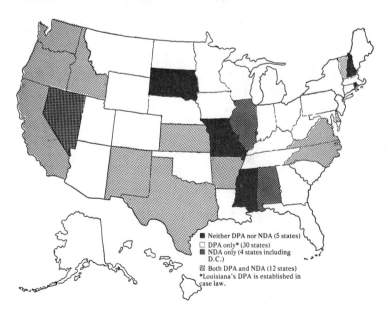

■ Neither DPA nor NDA (5 states)
□ DPA only* (30 states)
▨ NDA only (4 states including D.C.)
▨ Both DPA and NDA (12 states)
*Louisiana's DPA is established in case law.

Living Will Declaration
(*Text from Virginia Natural Death Act*)

To My Family, Physician, Lawyer, Clergyman and
all others whom it may concern:

     Declaration made this _____ day of _____, 19____ .
I, _____ willfully and voluntarily make known
my desire that my dying shall not be artificially prolonged under the circumstances set forth below, and do hereby declare:

     If at any time I should have a terminal condition and my attending
physician has determined that there can be no recovery from such condition and my death is imminent, where the application of life-prolonging
procedures would serve only to artificially prolong the dying process, I
direct that such procedures be withheld or withdrawn, and that I be permitted to die naturally with only the administration of medication or the
performance of any medical procedure deemed necessary to provide me
with comfort care or to alleviate pain.

     In the absence of my ability to give directions regarding the use of
such life-prolonging procedures, it is my intention that this declaration
shall be honored by my family and physician as the final expression of my
legal right to refuse medical or surgical treatment and accept the conse-
quences of such refusal.

     (Optional) I hereby designate _____ to make
treatment decisions for me in the event I am comatose or otherwise unable
to make decisions for myself.

     I understand the full import of this declaration and I am emotionally
and mentally competent to make this declaration.

_____

     The declarant is known to me and I believe him or her to be of sound
mind.

             (signed by two witnesses)

The following document goes beyond the previous one in two respects. First, it spells out exactly what control I have over my own treatment and second it specifies that should I be unconscious or otherwise unable to make decisions regarding treatment for more than 24 hours, that shall constitute a decision against life support or treatment for recovery. The 24-hour clause is appropriate to persons over 65. For younger persons a longer period of incapacity should be specified.

— Ernest

An Alternative Living Will
(As drafted and signed by Ernest Morgan)

I want to have some control over my own death. In the event of **any** illness I want to know whether any given treatment is for recovery or life support, or whether it is for comfort. And I want to be free to accept or decline any specific treatment. In the event of my incapacity to make such decisions, because of unconsciousness or other condition, for more than 24 hours, that circumstance shall constitute a decision against treatment directed toward recovery or life support.

When death does come I want to go as gracefully and as comfortably as possible, and not be held back by well-meaning medics and family.

Date _____ Signed _____

We accept and support Ernest's perspective in this matter:

(Signed by wife, children and personal physician)

It is important that one's actions be tempered by respect for the feelings of one's family. This need not mean submitting to the painful and expensive prolongation of life. A preferable alternative is to talk the matter over thoughtfully while one is in good health, and arrive at an understanding that gives the person control over his or her death without violating the feelings of other members of the family.

It is often helpful to approach the problem as a mutual one. Other members of one's family may, on serious reflection, want similar consideration for themselves.

Burial Boxes

Repeatedly people have asked where to buy, or how to build, simple burial boxes. The following information is intended primarily for families or groups who wish to carry out their own arrangements without a funeral director. Ordinarily, funeral directors expect to provide a casket unless some understanding has been arrived at to the contrary.

Boxes of Cabinet Quality: Sometimes people buy or build nicely handcrafted boxes in advance of need to use as furniture: a settee, linen chest, or a cabinet (by standing it on end with shelves inserted). Plans for making them, and in some cases the boxes as well, are available from the St. Francis Center, 1768 Church St. NW, Washington DC 20036 (price on request); from Dale Zamzow, Box 4610, Santa Clara CA 95054 ($5.95/blueprints); and from St. Leo League, Box 577, Newport RI 02840 (instructions/$3.50).

Corrugated Fiber Boxes: These can be made by any firm that makes corrugated fiber boxes, but their minimum order is generally large. If anyone knows of dealers handling them in small lots, please write to us.

Inexpensive Plywood Boxes: We offer here instructions for making four sizes of plywood boxes which are inexpensive, compact and easy to build. One group we know keeps on hand one each of all four sizes. These boxes are not suitable for body transportation by common carrier or for keeping an unembalmed body for any length of time. If used at a funeral they may be placed on a low bench or other support, covered by a cloth (pall).

	HOME-MADE BURIAL BOXES				
SIZES OF BURIAL BOXES	¾'' Plywood Cheap Grade		¼'' Plywood Cheap Grade		¾'' Plain Lumber (or Plywood)
	Bottom (1 needed)	Ends (2 needed)	Sides (2 needed)	Top (1 needed)	Side Strips (2 needed)
LARGE SIZE Outside: 6'6'' x 26'' x 16'' Inside: 6'4½'' x 24'' x 15''	6'4½'' x 25½''	26'' x 15¾''	6'4½'' x 15¾''	6'6'' x 26''	6'4½'' x 5''
MEDIUM SIZE Outside: 6' x 21'' x 13½'' Inside: 5'10½'' x 19'' x 12½''	5'10½'' x 20½''	21'' x 13¼''	5'10½'' x 13¼''	6' x 21''	5'10½'' x 5''
SMALL SIZE Outside: 5'6'' x 21'' x 13½'' Inside: 5'4½'' x 19'' x 12½''	5'4½'' x 20½''	21'' x 13¼''	5'4½'' x 13¼''	5'6'' x 21''	5'4½'' x 4''
CHILD SIZE Outside: 3'11'' x 16'' x 11'' Inside: 3'9½'' x 14'' x 10''	3'9½'' x 15½''	16'' x 10¾''	3'9½'' x 10¾''	3'11'' x 16''	3'9½'' x 3''

Home-Made Burial Boxes

Instructions: These four boxes can be made from two sheets of ¾'' plywood and 3½ sheets of ¼'' plywood. Order the necessary parts from the lumber yard, cut *accurately* to size. Anyone modestly experienced with tools can assemble the boxes.

Chart for Cutting Plywood Sheets: Two sheets of ¾'' 4'x8' plywood, cut as shown in the two diagrams below, will provide all the ¾'' plywood parts needed to build the four sizes of boxes listed above. The ¼'' plywood is simpler and needs no cutting chart, so we have simply explained below how it should be cut.

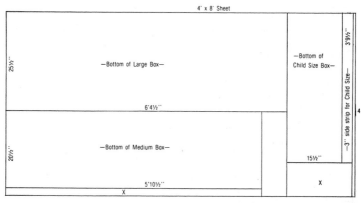

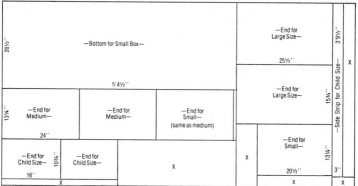

Cutting instructions for ¼'' plywood (No diagrams needed):

First Sheet (4'x8'): Top for Large box (6'6''x26''), and one side (6'4½'' x15¾''). Cut long way.
Top for Child Size (3'11''x16''). Cut from remaining end.

(continued)

Second Sheet: Top for Medium Size (6'x21''), and two sides (5'10½''x 13¾''). Cut long way.

Two sides for Child Size (3'9½''x10¾''). Cut from end piece.

Third Sheet: Top for Small Size (5'6''x21''), and two sides (5'4½''x13¼''). Cut long way.

A large end piece will be left over. This can be used to make an extra top and side of Child Size for possible future use.

Still Needed: The second side for the Large Size. If the lumber yard has part of a sheet from which this can be cut, fine. If not, a fourth sheet will be needed. In that case, the rest of the sheet can be cut into spare parts and stored with the boxes for possible later use.

Also Needed: Two side strips of ¾'' lumber for Large Size (5''x6'4½'').
    Two side strips of ¾'' lumber for Medium Size, (5''x5'10½'').
    Two side strips of ¾'' lumber for Small Size (4''x5'4½'').
(Side strips for Child Size were included in a previous cut.)

From the hardware store, get some 7/8'' nails, and some 4- and 8-penny box nails and four chest handles for each box. The handles should be of the kind that hang down when not in use and stay in horizontal position when lifted. Don't forget to get screws for these.

Assembly Diagram

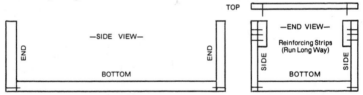

Nail a narrow strip to each side piece, flush with the edge and the end, using 4-penny nails. The good side of the plywood should be out.

Nail the side pieces to the bottom, using 7/8'' nails. The strips should be inside and at the top.

Nail the ends, with the good sides out, firmly to the bottom and to the side strips, using 8-penny nails, and the job is done.

The handles may be stored inside the box and screwed on when the box is used. Likewise, the cover may be tacked lightly in place until the box is needed, and then nailed firmly down with 7/8'' nails when the box is used.

The box, when loaded, should be moved with care to avoid pulling the ends away from the box. After the cover has been nailed down, however, the box is quite strong and can be handled freely. By using screws in the ends instead of nails, the box can be made quite strong without the lid.

When the box is used, two handles should be screwed to each end for ease in going through doors. They may be removed with a screwdriver and brought home from the crematory or cemetary for future use.

When a body is taken to the medical school in one of these boxes, it is customary to remove the body from the box and take the box home.

To save storage space, these boxes are so designed that the medium size can nest inside the large size, and the child size inside the small size.

The design for these boxes is based, with modifications, on ones used for years by the Burial Committee of the Yellow Springs Friends Meeting. They are sturdy, inexpensive, easy to build and compact to store. Since they have been modified from the original design—for the better, I hope—we will appreciate comments and criticisms from groups who use this design.

Burial Forms

The form shown (front and back) on the following pages was developed by the Burial Committee of the Yellow Springs (Ohio) Friends Meeting and has been in use, virtually unchanged, for thirty years. (Their term "burial" in this case is figurative. In practice the committee was concerned only with cremation or removal to a medical school.)

Each family wishing to be served by the committee was required to fill out a "Registration of Intent" for each member of the family, presumably *in advance* of need. This was done in duplicate, one copy being filed by the committee, the other retained by the family.

Very important, each family was expected to clear their plans in advance with all close relatives. Failure to do this commonly resulted in painful misunderstandings at the time of death.

About every five years the committee would review all the forms on file, to bring them up to date. The first time this was done by mailing the forms to the families, asking them to update them and return them. However, people don't like to think about death—especially their own death—and they put off reviewing the forms, with the result that many did not get returned. After that, the committee decided to update the forms by phone calls or by personal visits.

REGISTRATION OF INTENT OF SIMPLE BURIAL
Yellow Springs (Ohio) Friends Meeting

THIS FORM, filled out, also inclu‖ information for obituary and le‖ data for death certificate.

NAME _____

DATE FILLED OUT

Address _____

_____

County _____ S. S. No. _____

DATES REVIEWED

Date of Birth _____ Place _____

Father's Name _____

Mother's Maiden Name _____

I desire that, if circumstances permit at the time of my death, the Yellow Springs Monthly Meeti‖ of Friends shall carry out the arrangements set forth below.

Date _____   Signature _____

Witness _____   Witness _____

☐ I wish my body cremated.
☐ I wish my body given to a medical school.
  (See bequeathal form)
☐ I wish my eyes given to an eye-bank.

DISPOSAL OF REMAINS: Check which of the following dispositions of ashes you request: Left at crematory for disposal there. Delivered to one of the following:

(Names and addresses in order of preference)

FORM OF MEMORIAL SERVICE: Unless otherwise specified, the usual practice would be a memorial worship meeting at Rockford after the disposal of the body and with no expenditure for flowers. There will be no public viewing of the body. Please indicate any specific requests:

....

NEXT OF KIN: The following information is necessary to clear the Meeting's actions immediately on death of a participant. List next of kin in order of precedence:

NAME AND PERMANENT ADDRESS

1.

TEL.:

2.

TEL.:

3.

TEL..

Do you expect full understanding and cooperation on ‖ part of the above individuals?

A member of the Burial Committee will discuss with y‖ the circumstances requiring any qualified answer.

ENDORSEMENTS: We understand and are in accord with ‖ intent indicated above.

NAME	DATE
,	
,	

(Members of immediate family—next of kin)

FOLLOWING TO BE SIGNED AFTER DEATH OF REGISTRANT:

I authorize the Burial Committee of Yellow Springs Frien‖ Meeting to carry out the program indicated above.

SIGNATURE:

DATE:

TWO WITNESSES:

(OVER)

BIOGRAPHICAL DATA

(Suggest pencil for items subject to change)

Marital status _____ Wedding date _____

Usual Occupation _____ Business or Industry _____

Parents' Residence (if living) _____

Sisters' & Brothers' Residences _____

_____

_____

Children's Residences _____

_____

_____

Schools attended (Dates): _____

_____

When moved here _____

Organization, community projects, special achievements _____

_____

_____

_____

(The following information is required by law for the death certificate of a veteran.)

Name of war or dates of service _____

Type of Discharge _____ Date _____ Rank _____

Service (Army, Navy, etc.) _____ Organization (Regiment, Fleet, etc.) _____

Unit (as Company, Battery, Ship, etc.) _____

Branch (Infantry, Artillery, etc.) _____

(This data may be gotten from a veteran's discharge papers.)

(OVER)

Appendix VII / DIRECTORY OF MEMORIAL SOCIETIES

Continental Association of Funeral and Memorial Societies (CAFMS), 2001 S Street N.W., Suite 530, Washington, DC 20009. (202-745-0634). (See also Chapter VI, Memorial Societies.)

Memorial Society Association of Canada, Box 96, Station A, Weston, Ontario M9N 3M6.

Publications of CAFMS

The American Way of Death, Jessica Mitford, Fawcett Crest, 1979, 288 pp. $3.50. Updated version of 1963 classic.

Funerals: Consumers' Last Rights, Consumers Union, 1977, 334 pp. $7.00. Complete and practical information on funerals, cremation, body donation, and memorial societies.

Handbook for Funeral & Memorial Societies, CAFMS, 1976, 100 pp. $3.50. Essential how-to-do-it guide for organizing & running a memorial society.

"Last Rights ... an Alternative Way," describes memorial societies and includes directory. Pamphlet, single copies free.

"Directory of Memorial Societies in US and Canada." Single copies free.

"The Memorial Society," a description; pamphlet, single copies free.

"Information on Anatomical Gifts," fact sheet, single copies free.

"Facts about Cremation," fact sheet, single copies free.

"How to Organize a Memorial-Funeral Society," leaflet, single copies free.

"Putting My House in Order," 4-page form for listing all estate and funeral planning information needed by a person's heirs at time of death. 50¢.

Forms for Bequeathal to medical school, 60¢ each, 3 for $1.50.

Uniform Donor Cards, single cards free.

A Multitude of Voices: Funerals & the Clergy. Packet for leaders of all religious faiths. Includes booklet of funeral information; sample insert for Sunday/Sabbath bulletin or separate distribution; sample copy of "Smoothing the Way" guide & form for funeral planning; directory of memorial societies, poster for display. $2.00.

Helping. Packet for those providing care to the aging. Includes pamphlet with information and resource guide for providers; "Smoothing the Way" guide & form for funeral planning; memorial societies directory; poster for display. $1.00.

Where There's a Will. Materials for attorneys and advisors for assisting clients with wills or estate plans. Includes basic information about funeral decisions; "Smoothing the Way" funeral planning guide & form; memorial societies directory. $2.00.

Funeral Practices: Survey of State Laws & Regulations, 1980 survey of 24 consumer protection provisions in 50 states and D.C. Easy-to-use chart. $2.00.

Ordering Information

Make check or money order payable to "Memorial Society Fund." Payment must accompany order. Bulk prices available on request. Allow 4-6 weeks for delivery.

Directory of Funeral and Memorial Societies

U.S. Societies

ALABAMA: *Mobile:* The Azalea Funeral & Memorial Council, 302 Bay Shore Ave., Box 92 36607 (205-653-9092)

ALASKA: *Anchorage:* Cook Inlet Memorial Society, Box 10-2414 99510 (907-277-6001/272-7801)

ARIZONA: *Phoenix:* Valley Memorial Society, P.O. Box 3074, Scottsdale 85257 (602-990-3055)

Prescott: Mem. Soc. of Prescott, 335 Aubrey St. 86301 (602-778-3000)

Tucson: Tucson Mem. Soc., Box 12661 85732 (602-884-5099)

Yuma: Mem. Soc. of Yuma, Box 4314 85364 (602-726-8014)

ARKANSAS: *Fayetteville:* Northwest Arkansas Mem. Soc., 610 Henryetta, Springdale 72764 (501-751-5175)

Little Rock: Mem. Soc. of Central Arkansas, 12213 Rivercrest Dr. 72212 (501-225-7276)

CALIFORNIA: *Arcata:* Humboldt Funeral Society, Box 391, Rio Dell 95562 (707-822-1321)

Berkeley: Bay Area Funeral Soc., Box 264 94701 (415-841-6653)

Fresno: Valley Mem. Soc., Box 101 93707 (209-268-2181)

Los Angeles: Los Angeles Funeral Society, Inc., Box 44188, Panorama City 91412 (818-894-1551)

Modesto: Stanislaus Mem. Soc., Box 4252 95352 (209-523-0316)

Palo Alto: Peninsula Funeral and Mem. Soc., Box 60448A 94306 (415-321-2109)

Ridgecrest: Kern Mem. Soc., 1549 S. Gordon St. 93555

Sacramento: Sacramento Valley Mem. Soc., Inc., Box 161688, 3720 Folsom Blvd. 95816 (916-451-4641)

San Diego: San Diego Mem. Soc., Box 16336 92116 (619-284-1465)

San Luis Obispo: Central Coast Mem. Soc., Box 679 93401 (805-543-6133)

Santa Barbara: Channel Cities Mem. Soc., Box 424 93102 (805-569-1794)

Santa Cruz: Funeral & Mem. Soc. of Monterey Bay, Inc., Box 2900 95063 (408-462-1333)

Stockton: San Joaquin Mem. Soc., Box 4832 95204 (209-462-8739)

COLORADO: *Denver:* Rocky Mountain Mem. Soc., 1400 Lafayette St. 80218 (303-830-0502)

CONNECTICUT: *Groton:* Mem. Soc. of S.E. Conn. (Branch of M.S. of Greater New Haven), Box 825 06340 (203-445-8348)

Hartford: Mem. Soc. of Greater Hartford, 459 Firetown Rd., Simsbury 06070 (203-728-6609)

New Haven: Mem. Soc. of Greater New Haven, 60 Connelly Parkway, c/o

Co-op, Hamden 06514 (203-288-6463/ 488-6511)

Southbury: Southbury Branch of Greater New Haven Mem. Soc., 974-A Heritage Village 06488 (203-264-7564)

Westport: Mem. Soc. of SW Conn., 71 Hillendale Rd. 06880 (203-227-8705)

D.C.: *Washington:* Mem. Soc. of Metro Washington, 1500 Harvard St. N.W. 20009 (202-234-7777)

FLORIDA: *Cocoa:* Fun. & Mem. Soc. of Brevard County, Inc., Box 276 32923-0276 (305-459-0053/452-8608)

DeBary: Fun. Soc. of Mid-Florida, Box 262 32713 (305-668-6587)

Ft. Walton Beach: Mem. Soc. of N.W. Florida, P.O. Box 4122 32549-4122 (904-837-6559)

Ft. Myers: Fun. & Mem. Soc. of S.W. Florida, Inc., 6 E.First St., Box 6, Windmill Village, N. Ft. Myers 33903 (813-656-2022)

Gainesville: Mem. Soc. of Alachua County, 2015 N.W. 12th Rd. 32604 (904-376-7073)

Jacksonville: Jacksonville Mem. Soc., 6915 Holiday Rd. N. 32216 (904-724-3766)

Miami: Miami Mem. Soc., Box 557422, Ludlam Branch 33155 (305-667-3697)

Orlando: Orange County Mem. Soc 2903 Bridgegate Ct. 32822 (305-898-3621)

Pensacola: Fun. & Mem. Soc. of Pensacola & West Florida, 9759 Pickwood Drive 32514 (904-477-1912)

St. Petersburg: Suncoast-Tampa Bay Mem. Soc., 719 Arlington Ave. N. 33701 (813-898-3294)

Sarasota: Mem. Soc. of Sarasota, Box 5683 33579 (813-953-3740)

Tallahassee: Fun. & Mem. Soc. of Leon County, Box 20189 32304

Tampa: Tampa Mem. Soc., 3915 N. "A" St. 33609 (813-877-4604)

W. Palm Beach: Palm Beach Fun. Soc., Box 2065 33402 (305-833-8936)

GEORGIA: *Atlanta:* Mem. Soc. of Ga., 1911 Cliff Valley Way, N.E. 30329 (404-634-2896)

HAWAII: *Honolulu:* Fun. & Mem. Soc. of Hawaii, 200 N. Vineyard Blvd., Suite 403 96817 (808-538-1282)

ILLINOIS: *Bloomington:* McLean County Branch of Chicago Mem. Soc., 1613 E. Emerson 61701 (309-828-0235)

Carbondale: Mem. Soc. of Carbondale Area, 607 W. Owens St. 62901 (618-457-6240)

Chicago: Chicago Mem. Assn., 59 E. Van Buren St. 60605 (312-939-0678)

Peoria: Mem. Soc. of Greater Peoria, 908 Hamilton Blvd. 61603 (309-673-5391)

Rockford: Mem. Soc. of N. Illinois, Box 6131 61125 (815-964-7697)

Urbana: Champaign County Mem. Soc., 309 W. Green St. 61801 (217-384-8862

INDIANA: *Bloomington:* Bloomington Mem. Soc., 2120 N. Fee Lane 47401 (812-332-3695)

Ft. Wayne: Mem. Soc. of Northeast Indiana, 2923 Woodstock Ct. 46815 (219-484-4385)

Indianapolis: Indianapolis Mem. Soc., 5805 E. 56th St. 46226 (317-545-6005)

Valparaiso: Mem. Soc. of Northwest Indiana, 356 McIntyre Ct. 46383 (219-462-5701)

West Lafayette: Greater Lafayette Mem. Soc., Box 2155 47906 (317-463-9645)

IOWA: *Ames:* Central Iowa Mem. Soc., 1015 Hyland Ave. 50010 (515-239-2314)

Davenport: Illowa Mem. Fun. Soc. (formerly Blackhawk Mem. Soc.), P.O. Box 2689 52809 (319-359-0816)

Iowa City: Mem. Soc. of Iowa River Valley, 120 Dubuque St. 52240 (319-337-3019/9828)

KENTUCKY: *Lexington:* Mem. Soc. of Lexington, Inc., 3564 Clays Mill Rd. 40503 (606-223-1448)

Louisville: Mem. Soc. of Greater Louisville, 322 York St. 40203 (502-585-5119)

LOUISIANA: *Baton Rouge:* Mem. Soc. of Greater Baton Rouge, 8470 Goodwood Ave. 70806 (504-926-2291)

New Orleans: Mem. Soc. of Greater New Orleans, 1800 Jefferson Ave. 70115 (504-891-4055)

MAINE: *Auburn:* Mem. Soc. of Maine, Box 3122 04210 (207-786-4323)

MARYLAND: *Baltimore:* Mem. Soc. of Greater Baltimore, 3 Ruxview Court, Apt. 101 21204 (301-296-4657/467-8987)

Bethesda: Maryland Suburban Mem. Soc., c/o Bruce Bowman, 14Z3 Laurell Hill, Greenbelt 20770 (301-474-6468)

Columbia: Howard County Mem. Foundation, 10451 Twin Rivers Rd., Wilde Lake Village 21044 (301-730-7920 /997-1188)

Hagerstown: Mem. Soc. of Tri-

State Area, 15 S. Mulberry 21740 (301-773-3565)

MASSACHUSETTS: *Brockton:* Mem. Soc. of Greater Brockton, 325 W. Elm St. 02401

Brookline: Mem. Soc. of New England, 25 Monmouth St. 02146 (617-731-2073)

New Bedford: Mem. Soc. of Greater New Bedford, Inc., 71 Eighth St. 02740 (617-994-9686)

Orleans: Mem. Soc. of Cape Cod, Box 1346 02653 (617-255-3841)

Springfield: Springfield Mem. Soc. Box 2821 01101 (413-733-7874)

MICHIGAN: *Ann Arbor:* Mem. Advisory & Planning Service, 2030 Chaucer 48103 (313-761-7135)

Battle Creek: Mem. Soc. of Battle Creek, c/o Art Center, 265 E. Emmet St. 49017 (616-962-5362)

Detroit: Greater Detroit Mem. Soc. 4605 Cass Ave. 48201 (313-833-9107)

East Lansing: Lansing Area Mem. Planning Soc., Box 925 48823 (517-351-4081)

Flint: Mem. Soc. of Flint, Unitarian Church of Flint, G-2474 S. Ballenger Hwy. 48507

Grand Rapids: Mem. Soc. of Greater Grand Valley, Box 1426 49501

Kalamazoo: Mem. Soc. of Greater Kalamazoo, 315 W. Michigan 49006

Mt. Pleasant: Mem. Soc. of Mid-Michigan, Box 172 48858 (517-773-9548)

Reed City: Mem. Soc. of Reed City Area, 324 W. Todd St. 49677 (616-832-2812)

MINNESOTA: *Minneapolis:* Minn. Funeral & Mem. Soc., 900 Mt. Curve Ave. 55403 (612-374-1515). Outstate Minn.: 717 Riverside Drive, S.E., St. Cloud 56301 (612-252-7540)

MISSISSIPPI: *Gulfport:* Fun. & Mem. Soc. of the Miss. Gulf Coast, Box 7406 39501 (601-435-2284)

MISSOURI: *Kansas City:* Greater Kansas City Mem. Soc., 4500 Warwick Blvd 64111 (816-561-6322)

St. Louis: Mem. & Planned Funeral Soc., 5007 Waterman Blvd. 63108 (314-361-0595)

MONTANA: *Billings:* Mem. Soc. of Montana, 1024 Princeton Ave. 59102 (406-252-5065/1828)

Missoula: Five Valleys Burial Mem. Assn., 401 University Ave. 59801 (406-543-6952)

NEBRASKA: *Omaha:* Midland Mem. Soc., 3114 Harney St. 68131 (402-345-3039)

NEVADA: *Las Vegas:* Fun. & Mem. Soc. of S. Nevada, Inc., P.O. Box 1704 89125 (702-739-6979)

Reno: Mem. Soc. of W. Nevada, Box 8413, Univ. Sta. 89507 (702-322-0688)

NEW HAMPSHIRE: *Concord:* Mem. Soc. of N.H., Box 702 03301 (603-224-8913)

NEW JERSEY: *Cape May:* Mem. Soc. of South Jersey, Box 592 08204 (609-884-8852)

East Brunswick: Raritan Valley Mem. Soc., 176 Tices Lane 08816 (201-246-9620/572-1470)

Lincroft: Mem. Assn. of Monmouth Co., 1475 W. Front St. 07738 (201-741-8092)

Madison: Morris Mem. Soc., Box 156 07940 (201-540-1177)

Montclair: Mem. Soc. of Essex, Box 888 07043 (201-783-1145)

Paramus: Central Mem. Soc., 156 Forest Ave. 07652 (201-445-6008)

Plainfield: Mem. Soc. of Plainfield, Box 307 07061

Princeton: Princeton Mem. Assn., Box 1154 08540 (609-924-1604)

Toms River: Mem. Assn. of Ocean County, Box 1329 08753 (201-350-0228)

NEW MEXICO: *Albuquerque:* Mem. Assn. of Central N.M., Box 3251 87190 (505-266-1523)

Farmington: Four Corners Mem. and Fun. Soc., Box 1254 87410

Las Cruces: Mem. & Fun. Soc. of Southern N.M., P.O. Box 12132, Mesilla Pk. 88047

Los Alamos: Mem. & Fun. Soc. of Northern N.M., Box 520 87544 (505-662-2346)

NEW YORK: *Albany:* Albany Area Mem. Soc., 405 Washington Ave. 12206 (518-465-9664)

Binghamton: Southern Tier Mem. Soc., 183 Riverside 13905 (607-729-1641)

Buffalo; Greater Buffalo Mem. Soc, 695 Elmwood 14222 (716-885-2136)

Corning: Mem. Soc. of Greater Corning, Box 23, Painted Post 14870 (607-962-2690)

Hornell: Upper Genesee Mem. Soc., 79 Elm St. 14843 (716-593-1060)

Ithaca: Ithaca Mem. Soc., Box 134 14850 (607-272-5476)

New Hartford: Mohawk Valley

Mem. Soc., 28 Oxford Rd. 13413 (315-797-1955)

N.Y.C.: Community Fun. Soc., 40 E. 35th St. 10016 (212-683-4988)

N.Y.C.: Mem. Soc. of Riverside Church, 490 Riverside 10027 (212-749-7000)

Niagara Falls: Mem. Soc. of Niagara, 639 Main St. 14301 (716-745-3922)

Pomona: Rockland County Mem. Soc., Box 461 10970 (914-354-2917)

Port Washington: Mem. Soc. of Long Island, Inc., Box 303 11050 (516-627-6590/944-9035)

Poughkeepsie: Mid-Hudson Mem. Soc., 249 Hooker 12603 (914-471-5078)

Rochester: Rochester Mem. Soc., 220 Winton Rd. S. 14610 (716-461-1620)

Syracuse: Syracuse Mem. Soc., Box 67, Dewitt 13214 (315-474-4580)

Watertown: Mem. Soc. of Northern N.Y., c/o Schwerzmann, 1138 Harrison St. 13601

White Plains: Funeral Planning Assn. of Westchester, Rosedale Ave. & Sycamore Lane 10605 (914-946-1660)

NORTH CAROLINA: *Asheville:* Blue Ridge Mem. Soc., Box 2601 28801

Chapel Hill: Triangle Mem. & Fun. Soc., Box 1223 27514 (919-942-4427)

Greensboro: Piedmont Mem. & Fun. Soc., Box 16192 27406 (919-674-5501)

Laurinburg: Scotland County Fun. & Mem. Soc., Box 192 28352

Wilmington: Mem. Soc. of the Lower Cape Fear, P.O. Box 4262 28406

OHIO: *Akron:* Mem. Soc. of Akron Canton, 3300 Morewood Rd. 44313 (216-836-8094)

Cincinnati: Mem. Soc. of Greater Cincinnati, Inc., 536 Linton St. 45219 (513-281-1564)

Cleveland: Cleveland Mem. Soc., 21600 Shaker Blvd. 44122 (216-751-5515)

Columbus: Mem. Soc. of the Columbus Area, Box 14103 43214 (614-267-4946)

Dayton: Dayton Mem. Soc., 665 Salem Ave. 45406 (513-274-5890)

Toledo: Mem. Soc. of N.W. Ohio, 2210 Collingwood 43620 (419-475-4812)

Wilmington: Fun. & Mem. Soc. of Southwest Ohio, 66 N. Mulberry St. 45177 (513-382-2349)

Yellow Springs: Yellow Springs Branch of Mem. Soc. of Columbus Area 317 Dayton St. 45387 (513-767-1659)

Youngstown: Mem. Soc. of Greater Youngstown, 75 Jackson Drive, Campbell 44405 (216-755-8696)

OKLAHOMA: *Oklahoma City:* Mem. Soc. of Central Oklahoma, 600 N.W. 13th St. 73103 (405-232-9224)

Tulsa: Mem. Soc. of E. Okla., 2952 S. Peoria 74114 (918-743-2363)

OREGON: *Eugene:* The Emerald Mem. Assn., Box 667, Pleasant Hill 97455

Portland: Oregon Mem. Assn., 6220 S.W. 130th, #17, Beaverton 97005 (503-283-5500)

PENNSYLVANIA: *Bethlehem:* Lehigh Valley Mem. Soc., 701 Lechauweki Ave. 18015 (215-866-7652)

Erie: Thanatopsis Soc. of Erie, Box 3495 16508 (814-864-9300)

Harrisburg: Mem. Soc. of Greater Harrisburg, 1280 Clover Lane 17113 (717-564-4761)

Philadelphia: Mem. Soc. of Greater Philadelphia, 2125 Chestnut St. 19103 (215-567-1065)

Pittsburgh: Pittsburgh Mem. Soc., 605 Morewood 15213 (412-621-8008)

Pottstown: Pottstown Branch of Mem. Soc. of Greater Philadelphia, 1409 N. State St. 19464 (215-323-5561)

Scranton: Mem. Soc. of Scranton-Wilkes-Barre Area, Box 212, RD #6, Clarks Summit 18411 (717-586-8261)

State College: Mem. Soc. of Central Pa., 758 Glenn Rd. 16801 (814-277-7605)

RHODE ISLAND: *East Greenwich:* Mem. Soc. of Rhode Island, 119 Kenyon Ave. 02818 (401-884-5933)

SOUTH CAROLINA: *Charleston:* Mem. Soc. of Charleston, 16 Edenwood Ct. 29407 (803-556-7721)

TENNESSEE: *Chattanooga:* Mem. Soc. of Chattanooga, 3224 Navajo Dr. 37411 (615-899-9315)

Knoxville: East Tenn. Mem. Soc., Box 10507 37919 (615-523-4176)

Nashville: Middle Tenn. Mem. Soc 1808 Woodmont 37215 (615-383-5760)

Pleasant Hill: Cumberland Branch of East Tenn. Mem. Soc., Box 246 38578 (615-277-3795)

TEXAS: *Austin:* Austin Mem. & Burial Information Soc., Box 4382 78765

Beaumont: Golden Triangle Mem. Soc., Box 6136 77705 (713-833-6883)

College Station: Mem. Soc. of Bryan-College Station, Box 9078 77840 (713-696-6944)

Dallas: Dallas Area Mem. Soc., 4015 Normandy 75205 (214-528-3990)

El Paso: Mem. Soc. of El Paso, Box 4951 79914 (505-824-4565)

Houston: Houston Area Mem. Soc. 5210 Fannin St. 77004 (713-526-1571)

Lubbock: Lubbock Area Mem. Soc. Box 6562   79413 (806-792-0367)

San Antonio: San Antonio Mem. Soc., 7123 Thrushview, #6   78209

UTAH: *Salt Lake City:* Utah Mem. Assn., 569 S. 13th East   84102 (801-582-8687)

VERMONT: *Burlington:* Vt. Mem. Soc. Box 67   05401 (802-863-4701)

VIRGINIA: *Alexandria:* Mt. Vernon Mem. Soc., 1909 Windmill Lane 22307 (703-765-5950)

Arlington: Mem. Soc. of Arlington, 4444 Arlington Blvd. 22204 (703-892-2565)

Charlottesville: Mem. Planning Soc. of the Piedmont, 717 Rugby Rd. 22903 (804-293-8179/3133)

Oakton: Fairfax Mem. Soc., Box 130   22124 (703-281-4230)

Richmond: Mem. Soc. of Greater Richmond, 1000 Blanton Ave.   23221

Roanoke: Mem. Soc. of Roanoke Valley, Inc., Box 8001 24014 (703-774-9314)

Virginia Beach: Mem. Soc. of Tidewater, Box 4621   23454 (804-425-9258)

WASHINGTON: *Seattle:* People's Mem Assn., 2366 Eastlake Ave. E.   98102 (206-325-0489)

Spokane: Spokane Mem. Assn., Box 13613   99213 (509-924-8400)

WISCONSIN: *Milwaukee:* Fun. & Mem Soc. of Greater Milwaukee, 2618 N. Hackett Ave.   53211 (414-962-0500)

Racine: Fun. & Mem. Soc. of Racine & Kenosha, 625 College Ave. 53403 (414-634-0659)

River Falls: Western Wisconsin Funeral Soc., 110 N. 3rd   54022 (715-425-2052)

Sturgeon Bay: Mem. Soc. of Door County, c/o Hope United Church of Christ   54235 (414-743-2701)

Canadian Societies

ALBERTA: *Calgary:* Calgary Co-op Mem. Soc., 28 Norseman Pl. N.W. T2K 5M6 (403-274-5120)

Edmonton: Mem. Soc. of Edmonton & District, 7908 143rd St. T5R 0N6 (403-486-3321)

Grande Prairie: Mem. Soc. of Grande Prairie, Box 471 T8V 3A7

Red Deer: Mem. Soc. of Red Deer & District, Box 817 T4N 5H2 (403-346-3452/3598)

MANITOBA: *Winnipeg:* Manitoba Fun. Planning and Mem. Soc., 790 Banning St.   R3E 2H9 (204-783-8312)

NEW BRUNSWICK: *Fredericton:* Mem. Soc. of New Brunswick, Box 622 E3B 5A6 (506-455-3287)

NEWFOUNDLAND: *St. John's:* Mem. and Fun. Planning Assn. of Newfoundland, Box 9183 Station "B" A1A 2X9 (709-368-7784/5539)

NOVA SCOTIA: *Halifax:* Greater Halifax Mem. Soc., Box 291, Armdale B3L 4K1 (902-477-4192)

Sydney: Mem. Soc. of Cape Breton Box 934 B1P 6J4 (902-539-6536)

ONTARIO: *Guelph:* Mem. Soc. of Guelph, Box 1784 N1H 7A1 (519-822-7430)

Hamilton: Hamilton Mem. Soc., Box 164 L8N 3A2 (416-549-6385)

Kingston: Mem. Soc. of Kingston, Box 1081 K7L 4Y5 (613-542-727!)

Kitchener: Kitchener-Waterloo Mem. Soc., Box 113 N2G 3W9 (519-884-8317)

London: Mem. Soc. of London, Box 1729, Sta. A N6A 5H9 (519-472-0670)

Niagara Peninsula: Niagara Peninsula Mem. Soc., Box 2102, 4500 Queen St., L2E 6Z2 (416-354-6134)

Ottawa: Ottawa Mem. Soc., 4 Sherry Lane, Nepean K2G 3L5 (613-226-8689)

Peterborough: Mem. Soc. of Peterborough & District, Box 1795 K9J 7X6 (705-742-0550)

Sudbury: Mem. Soc. of Northern Ontario, Box 2563, Sta. A P3A 4S9 (705-673-5532)

Thunder Bay: Mem. Soc. of Thunder Bay, Box 501, Sta. F P7C 4W4 (807-683-3051)

Toronto: Toronto Mem. Soc., Box 96, Sta. A, Weston M9N 3M6 (416-241-6274)

Windsor: Mem. Soc. of Windsor, Box 481 N9A 6M6 (519-969-2252)

QUEBEC: *Montreal:* L'Association Funeraire de Montreal, Box 400, Sta. C H2L 4K3 (514-521-2815)

SASKATCHEWAN: *Lloydminster:* Lloydminster, Vermillion & District Mem. Soc., 4729 45th St. S9V 0H6 (306-825-3769)

Saskatoon: Mem. Soc. of Saskatchewan, Box 1846 S7K 3S2 (306-374-5190)

BRITISH COLUMBIA: *Vancouver:* Mem. Soc. of B.C., Room 410, 207 W. Hastings St. V6B 1J3 (688-6256)—*membership is pending*

Memorial Services

On the following pages are several memorial services, each of which has been selected for some feature that seemed especially interesting. They have been compiled by Ann Baty of the Bowling Green, Ohio Memorial Society. Each of the first seven was written for a particular person who had died. Of the others, one is a general type of service that can be used for anyone. It is followed by two committal services—one for burial and one for cremation. The children's "Good-bye Service" is not intended for a formal service but is meant to be used to help a child or children to cope with a grievous loss.

I. Service with Flower Communion

The memorial service for Esme Harold Naaman was prepared by a friend. Esme's death had ended several months of loving care given by friends who made it possible for him to die at home.

An order of service was mimeographed and folded into a booklet of ten pages plus cover. It contained the full text of all the selections that were used. It was mailed to friends and family who could not attend and served, for some, as a notice of Esme's death. The cover had his name and the dates of his birth and death with a pargraph about the kind of person he was.

After an interval of music by Bach and Brahms, as people gathered, the service began with these words: "We are a group of friends gathered together to pay loving tribute to Esme Naaman and to share with his family and each other our appreciation of a rare and remarkable human being."

Words written about him by a friend or two were read, as were a couple of letters that he had received (from brother and son) and which contained revealing sentiments. There were other readings: from *Voice of the Desert* by Joseph Wood Krutch, from *The Prophet* by Kahlil Gibran and from Kenneth L. Patton. There were intervals of music (Sibelius, Croft, Mozart, Bach) and a short eulogy. A statement of the kind of person Esme had been was read by the minister.

Finally a friend said, "We invite you to take a blossom in our diverse remembrances of Esme." To the accompaniment of Bach's "Vater Unser in Himmelriech," four friends passed shallow baskets of chrysanthemum blossoms in yellow, bronze and white as a flower communion; after that was a recitation of The Lord's Prayer and then a recessional by Bach.

The service was held in a Unitarian Church but was conducted by lay friends, rather than by the minister. The selections written by Kenneth L. Patton were *The Measure of Sorrow* and *Our Own Good-Byes*.

II. Service Using Writings of the Deceased

Marcos Romero was a very creative young man from South America. While attending college in the United States, he was killed in a motorcycle accident. His friends put together this memorial service, using Marcos' own writings. The short service was held in a room in one of the college halls, and it was conducted entirely by students, his friends.

A program was printed and titled "Remembering Marcos Romero, A Service of Readings and Reflections." Date and place of the service also were printed on the cover.

The service began with a reading by a friend, followed by this litany:

LOVE ONE ANOTHER
Support one another's efforts
LOVE ONE ANOTHER
Rejoice in another's fulfillment
LOVE ONE ANOTHER
Support each other through difficult times
LOVE ONE ANOTHER
Rejoice together in times of rejoicing
LOVE ONE ANOTHER

Friends read from Marcos' writings, then sang a song written for Marcos by a friend. "Morning Has Broken" was sung by the group (the words were printed on the program).

There was a benediction from Marcos' writings: "Life is a matter of doing whatever has to be done with as much love as possible. By love, I mean concentration and dedication of one's life. I find that it is not so important to plan for the future, but to love everything we do and to let go and flow as a river flows."

The service ended with the reading of a poem written by Marcos Romero, titled "Good-bye: Dedicated to All Those Friends of Mine Who Listen."

III. Service with Organ Music

This service was arranged by friends of the deceased and was conducted by them. Harold Thomas Marlow had cared for his mother for many years until she died; he never married. After his mother died, he spent his time and energy working for his church; he left everything he had to the church.

The church had an organ and an organist, and most of the music was played by the organist. The service:

Prelude   Trumpet Tune in C and Trumpet Tune in D   — Purcell

Opening Words   ''Reasons for a Funeral or Memorial Service''
— Rev. Roy Phillips

We do best in our present and later lives if, when one we love dies, we bring together those whose lives were touched significantly by the life of the one who has died. This is the reason for a funeral or a memorial service.

While such services have been understood in many varying ways, their human function is to set an experiential marker at the endpoint of life, to place a cairn at the conclusion of one human being's journey.

The cairns along a wilderness trail are built of earth rocks of various shapes and sizes. The memorial cairn at the end of a life is also a composite, but an experiential one. It is made up of the memories, the thoughts and the feelings of all who are gathered in the one place together. It is a recollection (a re-collection) of what was for a time together and is now scattered and scattering. Here is the one we knew. This is how our lives were touched by that life. Here is what we think and how we feel.

The words spoken in the literal funeral or memorial service are not themselves the marker. The spoken words are evokers of experiences—thoughts, feelings, memories—within the people of the gathered group. These experiences are the memorial cairn.

At the end of a life, we compose a symphony, an ordered creation whose notes and themes are the experiences of the people gathered. Themes dark and bright are sounded to recollect and to order the impact of the life of the one who had died—honestly, fully, tenderly—and in the spirit of thanksgiving for the quality of that lived life.

The words of a memorial service should strive to evoke remembrance, thanksgiving, a sense of the uniqueness of the person's life, a sense of the privilege of having known that person, a sense of loss, of sadness, a feeling of emptiness, of unsureness and a hint that the ending of this life is a rehearsal of what is to come for every one of us. The words should evoke a sense of trust in the slow, but steady, grace of healing and the affirmation that we can live on and will live on, blessed by that life and by the memory of the one who once was and is now gone, but who is and will be present in the world, and in us in mysterious and hidden ways.

Harold Thomas Marlow, scholar, churchman, friend, has died. We are gathered here to pay honor to his spirit and to the life he lived, and to consecrate his memory. The readings and music speak of him; reflect his spirit in life; reflect our feeling for him, and our feeling at this time.

Introit "Well-Tempered Clavichord" — Bach

Readings "A Celebration for George Sarton (final stanza)
— May Sarton
"On Death" — Kahlil Gibran

Solo "Jesu, Joy of Man's Desiring" — Bach

Invitation to Thought

(Words about Tom spoken by the minister, and
and ending with a short meditation)

Do you seek Tom Marlow? Why seek ye the living among the dead? All tombs are empty, signposts toward the silent mystery that is our origin and destiny. Seek the living among the living. Seek Tom in yourselves, in the patterns of your mind and memory, in the shape of the world made a little different by him, in the very rhythm of your heart of hearts. Amen.

Solo "Pathetique Sonata Andante Cantabile" — Beethovan

Eulogy (read by a boyhood friend)

Solo "Fur Elise" — Beethovan

Reading "There Are Men Too Gentle to Live Among Wolves"*
— James Kavanaugh

Music "Suite in C" — Bach

Closing Words

We, the living, have come together to ponder the death of one known to us, loved by us. We have come with sorrow that a good life should have to end. We have come with deep memories of our times with him, of joy and sorrow we shared with him, of the delightful and even the impatient moments we knew when he was with us. Here was a man, a man with hopes and dreams; a man with secret fears and unanswered questions; but a man with a zest for life and the strength to weather the storms which each of us must face. We, the living, give thanks that we have known Tom. We give thanks that he walked among us. We give thanks that he lived. Amen.

Postlude "St. Anthony Chorale" — Haydn-Brahms

Sources

The readings suggested in this service can be found in the following sources: May Sarton, *Collected Poems: 1930-1973,* Norton, 1974; Kahlil Gibran, *The Prophet,* Alfred A. Knopf; James Kavanaugh, *There Are Men Too Gentle to Live Among Wolves,* Dutton, 1970.

---

*Our apologies to the four-legged wolves. They are not the ones referred to in this poem. As Farley Mowatt says, "Never Cry Wolf"—unless you specify which kind.

IV. Service Held for a Teen-Aged Girl

Mary, sixteen, was killed while on vacation with her family. Her body was cremated with a private committal service.

When the family returned to their home, a memorial service was held in the United Methodist Church to which they belonged. Significant objects relating to Mary, things she prized, graced the chancel area.

Music significant to the family, including "Bridge Over Troubled Water," was played.

The pastor spoke sentences of hope and comfort from the Scriptures, and he read the Twenty-Third Psalm. He prayed, and the congregation prayed The Lord's Prayer in unison. They sang "Precious Lord."

The youth minister read portions of the eighth chapter of Romans and preached on the text, "The Spirit Himself Intercedes for Us with Sighs Too Deep for Words."

A friend sang "One Day at a Time."

Those present were invited to share their thoughts about Mary with one another as the spirit moved them. (Mary's high school English teacher read from Mary's writings. One of her brothers read a poem she had written. Her father and mother, referring to the objects in the room and recent conversations with Mary, expressed their grief and hope and their need for the community of love.)

The congregation sang "Joy Is Like the Rain."

They were invited to come forward and stand with family for Holy Communion. The minister took the bread and a cup, gave thanks, broke the bread—a loaf baked by a friend—and gave the bread and the cup to the people, who served one another hand to hand.

They sang "Amazing Grace," received the benediction, and sang "Shalom"—the congregation's customary closing song. The people spontaneously shared their love with the family, and then gradually dispersed.

> — from *Abingdon Funeral Manual*
> by Perry H. Biddle, Jr.
> Quoted with permission, Abingdon Press, Nashville TN

V. A Memorial Walk

A "Memorial Walk" was held for Steve Persons on a Sunday afternoon at the small golf course in the Mobile Home Park where he had been living. Steve had been an avid golfer for many years and many friends knew him best in the golf setting.

Steve's friends gathered at the designated entrance to a path that followed the edge of the greens toward the Mobile Home Park club house just two short blocks away. The family arrived and led the group along the path to a mid-point bordering the golf course, where a large oak tree spread its branches. Here they stopped. Some sat on a bench beneath the tree as the friends grouped themselves around the family. While those in attendance absorbed the beauty of the golf course where Steve had spent so many happy hours, his nephew spoke some words of greeting, then gave a biographical sketch of Steve's life. Two of Steve's favorite songs were played on a cassette tape recorder, after which a friend spoke briefly and respectfully about Steve's interests and accomplishments in the world of music. The family then led the walk to the club house entrance where they turned and greeted their friends who passed through the door into the building.

Inside, the group found seats in the informal lounge. Simple refreshments were served while favorite classical piano selections were played. People were able to relax comfortably to talk to each other and the family, and especially to talk with relatives from afar whom they had not seen for a long time.

This memorial service, though quite simple, was very comforting and filled with love. Real support and sympathy was shown to the family as they and their friends exchanged incidents, anecdotes and many remembrances about their beloved Steve throughout the rest of the afternoon.

VI. An Unstructured Service Held in a Farmyard

This was a service held for Tom Blank. He had grown up on a farm near a small city. He had lived in the same community all of his life. After he died, his brother arranged for a memorial service held outdoors in the farmyard, just as Tom once, years before, had said he'd like it to be.

Chairs were carried out onto the lawn; a table of soft drinks was set up at one side. A rowboat that Tom had enjoyed using on the river in his playtime hours was filled with garden and field flowers; it also held a self-portrait Tom had painted.

There were some prepared readings, but guests were invited to, and did, speak as the spirit moved them to do so about their love for Tom.

VII. A Quaker Service

A man describes the unplanned service for his wife as "The most beautiful and meaningful memorial service I ever attended."

She had become a very active and devoted Friend (Quaker) after having been a Catholic for more than sixty years. She died very early on a Saturday morning. A friend of hers went all over the campus (where they taught) and spread the word to all her friends, asking them to attend the regular Sunday morning service of the Friends Meeting—even if they were not Quakers. And they did. "In the traditional Quaker manner," the gentleman writes, "all sat around in a circle with only a rug and a large candle in the center, and a number of those who knew her spoke feelingly of what she had meant to them, and what she had done for other people. There were no rehearsed speeches, no eulogy by someone who had to be briefed. The testimonies were given from first-hand experience and from the heart . . . and at the end, all joined hands with their neighbors, in accordance with their custom.''

VIII. *Love Memorial for Our Son* [as described by his mother]

Scott had been a skydiver for ten years, with over 2,000 jumps and twenty-four hours of freefall. His skydiving had taken him all over the United States and Europe. He had always assured me, when I worried, that he was safer in the air than driving on the highway.

We were totally unprepared, therefore, for the news of his death 1,000 miles away from home. We didn't know what to do. We were aware of the local Memorial Society; we weren't members, but we knew people who were. We called them and got the telephone number of the Memorial Society in Tampa, where Scott had been killed. We called there, and they put us in touch with a funeral home. Scott's body was cremated. Everyone was most helpful and thoughtful. The ashes were brought back with Scott's belongings and his car.

We wanted to have a very special and beautiful memorial service for our son; he was a very special and beautiful person. We also wanted his ten-year-old daughter to have something beautiful to remember. At first we weren't sure just how to go ahead, then suddenly ideas began coming. I believe Scott must have been helping me; even the poem we used for a memorial card was the first one I looked at.

All our family and friends helped. There was no time to get printing done, nor to order special paper. Our daughter made up a sample memorial card, and we had quick-print copies made on stationery.

The urn, with ashes, was placed in a cut-crystal bowl surrounded by red and white rose petals with a tall basket of red and white carnations on each side for the service in the Catholic church. From the church everyone went to the park on the river, where Scott had been best man at his brother's wedding some months before. A service was held there, while Scott's skydiving team flew over the river and scattered the ashes together with a bushel of rose petals. A red or white carnation was given to each of those gathered there to cast upon the water with their special love and a prayer for Scott. Sheri, Scott's daughter, cast a white rose bud.

Since there were a great many people from out of town, we asked everyone to come to our house for refreshments, which had been brought in and were served by our wonderful friends and neighbors. We all shared our memories of Scott; his skydiving awards were presented to us at that time.

IX. Recognition of Death

(Adapted from *The Book of Celebration* by Duke T. Gray and from ''A Humanist Funeral Service'' by Corliss Lamont and distributed by the Memorial Society of London, Box 4595, London, Ontario N5W 5J5.)

This service may be used either for a funeral service, with the body present, or for a memorial service following burial or cremation. Either service may be done in a church or elsewhere. It is designed to include congregational participation if copies can be made available so that those gathered can take part. This is an important way of helping to evoke the grief and hope which must have its expression. Otherwise, the minister or someone else may simply read the unison or responsive parts.

Music (optional)

Responsive Reading

Reader: Oh, Death, where is your sting?
Oh, Grave, where is your victory?

Unison: Peace be with us.

Reader: We must all die, and are as water spilt on the ground, which cannot be gathered up again.

Unison: Peace be with us.

Reader: Set me as a seal upon your heart, as a seal upon your arm: for love is strong as death.

Unison: Peace be with us.

Reader: Blessed are those who mourn, for they shall be comforted.

Unison: Peace be with us.

Reader: Blessed are you that weep now, for you shall laugh.

Unison: Peace be with us.

Reader: I have set before you life and death, blessing and cursing: Therefore choose life, that both you and your descendents may live.

Unison: Peace be with us.

Reader: And now abide faith, hope and love, these three; but the greatest of these is love.

The Welcome

Let us call to memory the dead yet ever-living who have passed the doors beyond which we cannot see. They dwell at peace in the halls of memory whose hallowed treasure it is ours to keep, from this day forward.

We have gathered in this place to do honor and praise to the life and memory of _____. We have gathered to offer thanksgiving and gratitude that one such as he/she has lived among us. We have gathered in celebration of death, and in so doing, in celebration of life—for life and death are one, even as the river flows to the sea.

(A candle may be lighted.)

Opening Prayer (in unison)

> Holy Spirit of Life, and of peace in death,
>> lift our sorrows
>
> Beloved memory and fragile hope,
>> heal the wounds of our mortal loss.
>
> Indestructible remembrance, in whom the spirits of the
>> departed do rest from their labors:
>
> We bless you for the memory of those most dear to us,
>> who have lived in joy and departed in peace.
>
> May we follow the best in them, and, truly loving and
>> serving the gifts they gave us,
>
> Be gathered with them into the life abundant,
>> against whose very richness
>> the forces of death cannot prevail. Amen.

The Circle of Life

Reader: To everything there is a season

Unison: And a time to every purpose under heaven:

Reader: A time to be born, and a time to die;

Unison: A time to plant, and a time to harvest;

Reader: A time to kill, a time to heal;

Unison: A time to break, and a time to build;

Reader: A time to weep, and a time to laugh;

Unison: A time to mourn, and a time to dance;

Reader: A time to cast away stones, and a time to bring stones together;

Unison: A time to embrace, and a time to be apart;

Reader: A time to get, and a time to lose;

Unison: A time to keep silence, a time to speak;

Reader: We should rejoice in our works, for that is our portion;

Unison: Cast your bread upon the waters; for you shall find it after many days.

— Ecclesiastes

Music (if desired)

Readings

(Readings, an address or remarks, and/or eulogy or biographical sketch)

In Memory of W.B. Yeats (final stanza)   — W.H. Auden

On Death from **The Prophet**   — Kahlil Gibran

Closing Prayer

Now the work is left to us, the living, to carry forth the beauty and joy of that life which has been taken from us. Where we weep, he/she would have us laugh. Where we mourn, he/she would have us rejoice. But we know that he/she will forgive us our grief, for to grieve is to love, to love is to cherish, and to cherish is to give praise and thanksgiving for the life which has blessed us all. To that life we pray courage and strength, that our frailty be forgiven,

our sorrows redeemed, the wounds of our loss healed, in the sure
knowledge that life moves forward and does not tarry with yesterday, and that the life before us beckons to greater glory as the only
memorial that is fitting and just. Amen.

X. Committal Services

A Committal Service for Cremation: Most crematories have an adjacent
chapel or an anteroom in which people may gather for a brief ceremony of
committal just before the cremation process begins:

In committing the body of ——————— to the flames, we do so
with deep reverence for that body as the temple, during life, of a
unique and beloved personality. Through the purifying process of
fire, this body now becomes transformed into the more simple and
ultimate elements of our universe. Fire is, itself, one of the great
forces of Nature.

"Fruit-Gathering"   — Sir Rabindranath Tagore
(See "Selected Readings," pages 136, 142.)

To the flame, then, we give finally the body of our friend with
the full and certain knowledge that, in the words of Socrates, "No
evil can befall a good man either in life or after death."

Benediction

Let us depart in peace, and look to the morning, assured that
tomorrow the Sun will rise again.

Life gives, and Life takes away; blessed be life, above all,
forever. Amen.

Alternative Benediction

Now, for us, the living,
may the love of friends,
the radiance of memory,
the fellowship of hope,
and the life abundant
fill us with all strength and peace,
that we may greet the breaking
of tomorrow's dawn
with praise. Amen.

An Interment Service for Burial: This is a service held at the grave site at the
time of burial; sometimes it is called a "graveside."

Opening Words   — Philippians 4

Whatsoever things are true,
Whatsoever things are honest,
Whatsoever things are just,
Whatsoever things are pure,
Whatsoever things are lovely,

Whatsoever things are of good report:
>if there be any virtue,
>and if there be any praise,
Think on these things.

>— I Corinthians 13

We know in part, and we prophesy in part.
But when that which is perfect is come,
>that which is in part shall be done away.
For now we see through a glass darkly;
>but then face to face;
Now I know in part; but then shall I know
>even as also I am known.

Prayer

Reader: In the midst of life, we are in death.
>Let us know full well that the spirit of our beloved dwells now in our hearts;
>Let us seek the courage, in love, to carry forward his/her memory in the lives we now lead.

Unison: Holy Spirit of Life, receive from us the person of ____.
>Let the best which was in him/her, be renewed in strength in us.
>May we now give to others the love that we no longer can give to him/her,
>For the lives we lead are now his/her honor and memorial.
>He/she would bless our sorrows with courage.
>May our time of pain issue in larger peace.
>He/she would wish it so;
>>So let it be. Amen.

Burial

For as much as the spirit of our brother/sister dwells no more in this mortal form, we commit the body to the ground, earth to earth, ashes to ashes, dust to dust; in the sure knowledge that his/her life continues in us, and that his/her works abide upon the earth. The torch he/she lit, we now carry forward, as also others will pass along ours.

>A flower may be tossed into the grave.

>>Down gently down
>>Softer to sleep
>>Than bed of night
>>From the littleness
>>Go.

>>Down gently down
>>Wider to wake
>>Than need of Sun
>>Into the greatness
>>Go.

XI. A Good-Bye Ceremony for Children

This ceremony was developed in a workshop on celebrations. This workshop tried to create ceremonies for those special situations that are important in our lives, but that are not customarily noted with a ceremony. One group chose to develop an observance to mark the death of a child's pet, but as they talked about, they realized that there are other deaths that might affect a child very deeply—not the devastating loss of a parent or sibling; that would be a different problem altogether. They were thinking of those incomprehensible, bewildering deaths, such as the death of a friend, of a good neighbor, of a slightly known or distant relative, of a teacher.

This ceremony is intended to help a child cope with grief and bewilderment and outrage. It can easily be held at home, but could be held in a schoolroom. It can be conducted by parents (or a parent) for a single child, or for several children. It is important that the expressions be honest—use words like death, sorrow, grief—not euphemisms. It's all right to cry.

> Begin with a statement of purpose, such as, "We've gathered together, today, to remember, with love, our friend, Jill, who has died. All living things must die, as we, too, will someday die. It makes us sad that this is so, but nothing lives forever."
>
> Read a poem, or have some music.
>
> Light a candle. "We light this candle; the light will symbolize for us Jill's life, as we think of how much we loved her. Although our sadness is great, we also think how glad we are that she lived, and we are thankful that we knew her, for we had happy times together. If we had some bad times, too, they aren't important now. We loved her; she was a good friend, we'll miss her very much."
>
> Music, or read a poem.
>
> Candlelighting Service: Provide several small candles, and arrange it so that each one can safely be left standing near the large candle—perhaps on a metal tray or in a tray of damp sand. Each child takes a candle, and lighting it at the large candle, says, "I remember . . . (something to do with Jill)," then places the small burning candle near the large burning candle.
>
> Extinguish the large candle, saying something like, "Jill, herself, has died, but memories of her, symbolized by these smaller candles, keep on glowing in our hearts and minds, just as the candles keep on glowing." Do not extinguish the candles, let them burn down, or, if the children are going to leave, let them leave while the candles are still burning.
>
> If this is a ceremony for a pet, it could end with burial.
>
> To use flowers instead of candles, have a large bouquet from which each child takes a flower as memories are recalled.

The children should understand, from what you say to them that, although the flowers will fade and die, because nothing living lasts forever, their memories will live on in their minds.

Selected Readings[1]

The following readings are offered for use in planning memorial, funeral, and commitment services. They are intended to supplement Biblical and other materials commonly available in reference works for clergy of various faiths.

Wise selection is the key to the effective use of readings. The sensibilities and wishes of the family as they plan the service should be the determining factor.

The readings offer perspective, too, to those contemplating their own death, or reflecting on past bereavement. They can be a source of inspiration and understanding for all students of death education.

General

> We meet here in the presence of death to do homage to the Spirit of Life. We would fain make this hour Love's hour and these simple rites Love's confessional. For it is Love's tribute that we come to offer here today.
>
> Our voices may be the voices of grief, but the language after which grief gropes is the language of Love. And we who gather here come in Love's name to express, for those whose lives have been bereft of Love's visible presence, a calm and abiding trust in Love's immortality and consecrating power.
>
> — Robert Terry Weston

> No one entering this world can ever escape sadness. Each in his turn must bear his burdens, though he be rich or poor, and in his turn bid his loved ones farewell as they set out upon life's ventures. Each one must suffer that sad farewell when loved ones embark on the last voyage, and each in turn must himself take that final journey into the dark.
>
> But to those who make this life a pledge to light and spirit there comes the assurance of a victory that shall redeem life's pain. Though our spirit be but the feeble glow of a candle, there is no dark that it cannot pierce. For him who keeps the candle burning bravely to the end, death is not defeat for light goes on.
>
> — Robert Terry Weston

> Bitter is the sorrow of bereavement, yet when a loved one passes, remember then the blessing we have received: rejoice that even for so brief a period our life has been enriched and deepened beyond the power of anything to destroy, for never beauty touched the heart of man without creating something eternal.
>
> — Robert Terry Weston

> And yet I say unto you, be of good courage, for although you may not escape sadness, it is because the life that has departed was rich and sweet that you are sad, and whatever has worth and

dignity and beauty is not lost. Nay, this is the testimony not only of the ages since the dawn of time, but this is the message of the test-tube and the telescope, even as prophets have proclaimed and poets sung, that nothing is ever lost, but that all things change and move throughout eternity. And dare we not believe that life itself shall be conserved, though bodies die and pass into the earth: yea, and that spirit through the crucible of mortality is not destroyed but purified and enriched and made more great?

— Robert Terry Weston

Gitanjali—87

In desperate hope I go and search for her in all the corners of my room; I find her not.

My house is small and what once has gone from it can never be regained.

But infinite is thy mansion, my lord, and seeking her I have come to thy door.

I stand under the golden canopy of thine evening sky and I lift my eager eyes to thy face.

I have come to the brink of eternity from which nothing can vanish—no hope, no happiness, no vision of a face seen through tears.

Oh, dip my emptied life into that ocean, plunge it into the deepest fullness. Let me for once feel that lost sweet touch in the allness of the universe.

— Rabindranath Tagore

Gitanjali—84

It is the pang of separation that spreads throughout the world and gives birth to shapes innumerable in the infinite sky.

It is this sorrow of separation that gazes in silence all night from star to star and becomes lyric among rustling leaves in rainy darkness of July.

It is this overspreading pain that deepens into loves and desires, into sufferings and joys in human homes; and this it is that ever melts and flows in songs through my poet's heart.

— Rabindranath Tagore

Gitanjali—90

"On the day when death shall knock at thy door,
    what wilt thou offer him?
"Oh, I will set before my guest the full vessel of
    my life—I will never let him go with empty hands.
"All the sweet vintage of my autumn days and summer nights,
    all the earnings and gleanings of my busy life
    will I place before him at the close of my days
    when death will knock at my door."

When I finished she remarked that her vessel was full.

— Rabindranath Tagore

Crossing the Bar

Sunset and evening star,
   And one clear call for me!
And may there be no moaning of the bar,
   When I put out to sea,

But such a tide as moving seems asleep,
   Too full for sound and foam,
When that which drew from out the boundless deep
   Turns again home.

Twilight and evening bell,
   And after that the dark!
And may there be no sadness of farewell,
   When I embark;

For though from out our bourne of Time and Place
   The flood may bear me far,
I hope to see my Pilot face to face
   When I have crossed the bar.

— Alfred, Lord Tennyson

Fruit-Gathering: XLVI

The time is past when I could repay
her for all that I received.

   Her night has found its morning and
thou hast taken her to thy arms: and
to thee I bring my gratitude and my
gifts that were for her.

   For all hurts and offences to her I
come to thee for forgiveness.

   I offer to thy service those flowers
of my love that remained in bud when
she waited for them to open.

— Rabindranath Tagore

Fruit-Gathering: XLIX

The pain was great when the strings
were being tuned, my Master!

   Begin your music, and let me forget
the pain; let me feel in beauty what
you had in your mind through those
pitiless days.

   The waning night lingers at my
doors, let her take her leave in songs.

   Pour your heart into my life strings,
my Master, in tunes that descend from
your stars.

— Rabindranath Tagore

In Memoriam: LIII

Oh yet we trust that somehow good
  Will be the final goal of ill,
  To pangs of nature, sins of will,
Defects of doubt, and taints of blood;

That nothing walks with aimless feet;
  That not one life shall be destroy'd,
  Or cast as rubbish to the void,
When God hath made the pile complete;

That not a worm is cloven in vain;
  That not a moth with vain desire
  Is shrivel'd in a fruitless fire,
Or but subserves another's gain.

Behold, we know not anything;
  I can but trust that good shall fall
  At last—far off—at last, to all,
And every winter change to spring.

So runs my dream: but what am I?
  An infant crying in the night:
  An infant crying for the light:
And with no language but a cry.
                — Alfred, Lord Tennyson

O God, eternal spirit of love and righteousness, through whose constant presence in our hearts we are made strong, and by whom we live, we come unto thee in this time of sorrow, and we are sustained by thine indwelling presence.

Thou teachest us to be reconciled unto sorrow; thou turnest sorrow into a universal sympathy and compassion. Trusting in thee we learn not merely to endure but to rejoice in life as a far more eternal and abiding thing than human flesh.

Not for ourselves alone, but for all who suffer and are afflicted by grief, we pray, that consciousness of thine eternity of fulfillment may uplift and sustain, and thy compassion minister to them through human hands.

May we learn to be glad for that which has been, not as something taken away but as something given to us even if for a brief time, through which we have been blessed. Teach us, we pray, to rejoice again, to share all beauty we have known, all love, all hope, all faith, and to be grateful for thy tender hand which at the end bringeth release in peace and blessed sleep.
                — Robert Terry Weston

I had rather think of those I have loved and lost as having returned to earth, as having become a part of the elemental wealth of the world, I would rather dream of them as unconscious dust; I would rather dream of them as laughing in the stream, floating in the clouds, bursting in light upon the shores of other worlds; I would rather think of them as the lost visions of a forgotten night, than to have even the faintest fear. . . . But as for me, I will leave the dead where nature leaves them. Whatever flower of hope springs in my heart I will cherish; I will give it breath of sighs and rain of tears.

R.G. Ingersoll, "The House of Death"

O thou, who art the inspirer of the faith that burns ever more brightly within the souls of men, unto thee do we turn in this time of testing. Within us do well up the great mysteries of the ages. The unanswered questions of all saddened hearts are on our lips. We would be assured and comforted if that might be within the power of our hearts to know and understand. But as we pause to honor a memory made beautiful by life, we pray only that our faith be strengthened by the faith that was so strong in him.

Maker of Mysteries, guide thou us whose spiritual vision is dim and uncertain. As the joy of close comradeship is withdrawn, do thou come with thy divine fellowship and renew our confidence in the everlasting life of the spirit of man.

— Francis G. Ricker

Mourn Not the Dead

Mourn not the dead that in the cool earth lie
Dust unto dust—
The calm, sweet earth that mothers all who die
As all men must;

But rather mourn the apathetic throng—
The cowed and meek
Who see the world's great anguish and its wrong
And dare not speak!

— Ralph Chaplin

A Scriptural Message for Use in a Memorial Service
by Rev. Philip Nordstrom (adapted)

God is our refuge and strength, our constant help in every sorrow;
Therefore we will not fear even though this earthly dust be
removed and be carried into the Eternal Sea,
For therein is a river whose fountains gladden the City of God,
the holy temples of his dwelling place.

Come behold now this work of the Lord, what transformations
he hath wrought on this earth, in this holy clay:
He hath made an end to this transitory struggle,
He hath unbent this bow, and shattered the shaft,
And he hath refined as in fire, this mortal chariot unto immortality.[1]

Comfort ye, comfort ye, my people, saith your God.
Speak ye comfortably to Jerusalem and say unto her
that her iniquity is pardoned.
For he shall lead his flock like a shepherd,
He shall carry the lambs in his arms
and gently lead those that are with young.

Have you not known?
Have you not heard that the everlasting God,
the creator of the ends of the earth
fainteth not, neither is weary.
For he giveth power to the faint and to them that have no might
He increaseth strength.
They shall walk and not faint,
they shall run and not be weary,
they shall mount up with wings as eagles.[2]

Behold, I will not leave you comfortless, but I will come unto you,
and I will make my abode with you,
and will come in and sup with you.[3]
In this world, ye shall have tribulation
but be of good cheer, I have overcome the world.[4]
My peace I give unto you;
not as the world gives, give I unto you.[5]
Behold! I will give you the oil of gladness
instead of mourning,
and sorrowing and sighing shall be done away.[6]

Come unto Me, all ye that labor and are heavy laden
and I will give you rest.
Take my yoke upon you and learn of me,
for I am meek and lowly in heart,
for my yoke is easy and my burden is light.[7]
Incline your ear, and come unto me,
hear, and your soul shall live.[8]

Remember that the eternal God is thy refuge
and underneath are the everlasting arms.

Comfort ye! Comfort ye, my people!
Says your God.

---

[1]Based on Psalm 46. [2]Isaiah 40:1-2, 11, 28-31. [3]John 14:18, 23. [4]John 16:33. [5]John 14:27. [6]Isaiah 61:3. [7]Matthew 11:28-30. [8]Isaiah 56:3.

For a Child

     Dear little child, released now from the burden of pain and sickness, we bless thee that thou hast shared thy life with us. Thou hast taught us depths and glorious truths of life that we should not have known but for thee. Through thee we have found insights into the hearts of men, we have dreamed dreams and seen visions which though they may never be fulfilled have forever lifted life for us above the commonplace. Thou hast given us the privilege of looking into life's holy of holies; through thee we have had a glimpse of Paradise; we have shared the knowledge and the glory of life's richest moments. Through thee life has become greater and deeper than else it had ever been. We bless thee as thou hast blessed us.

                                         — Robert Terry Weston

     In the flesh there is no continuing life, for things that are of flesh must perish after the way of flesh; yet there is no spirit, however weak or faint, however young, but leaves its glow upon the world; no spirit, however long or short its sojourn here, but speaks of greater and enduring life through its own sublime mystery and beauty. The spirit is of the nature of eternity: even as it smiles upon us here, suddenly there is a light about our heads and life is changed. So this bright spark of the eternal fire is not lost in death. The first brave smile of the tiniest babe kindles a warmth in other hearts that shall never die. Though death strike sorrow to our hearts, the glory of that smile still lingers within, to outlive sorrow and bind us to all childhood with enfolding love.

                                         — Robert Terry Weston

For the Aged

     Beautiful are the youth whose rich emotions flash and burn, whose lithe bodies filled with energy and grace sway in their happy dance of life; and beautiful likewise are the mature who have learned compassion and patience, charity and wisdom, though they be rarer far than beautiful youth. But most beautiful and most rare is a gracious old age which has drawn from life the skill to take its varied strands: the harsh advance of age, the pang of grief, the passing of dear friends, the loss of strength, and with fresh insight weave them into a rich and gracious pattern all its own. This is the greatest skill of all, to take the bitter with the sweet and make it beautiful, to take the whole of life in all its moods, its strengths and weaknesses, and of the whole make one great and celestial harmony.

                                         — Robert Terry Weston

For a Parent

Blessed are they who rear their families in honor and in gentleness, who live courageous and upright lives, who live life in its fullness, do their part, and then at eventide retire to rest.

Though pain be in the heart, let none grieve, for here a gentle soul has cast its glow upon us, and like the glory of an autumn sun, has lit the world with kindness through its day, and at the close has gently sunk to rest.

Rather rejoice for that which (she) has given, the light we know and treasure still within our hearts, a light we trust still shineth beyond the distant peaks (this world's horizon), for life goes on, and spirit knows no death.

— Robert Terry Weston

For Burial Commitment Services

Requiem

Fall softly, O thou coat of winter snow, and
    keep our loved one warm;
Kiss him gently, sun and rain, in the quiet of
    his rest;
Watch over him, wind and stars, in the silence
    of the night;
Grow thou to cover him, grass and flowers,
    and make beautiful his couch,
And thou, Great Spirit of Love and Peace, take
    him into thine arms and lull him to rest
    forevermore. Amen.

— Rev. John G. MacKinnon

Deep wet moss and cool blue shadows
    Beneath a bending fir,
And the purple solitude of mountains,
    When only the dark owls stir—
Oh, there will come a day, a twilight,
    When I shall sink to rest
In deep wet moss and cool blue shadows
    Upon a mountain's breast,
And yield a body torn with passions,
    And bruised with earthly scars,
To the cool oblivion of evening,
    Of solitude and stars.

— Lew Sarett

Song

She's somewhere in the sunlight strong,
Her tears are in the falling rain,
She calls me in the wind's soft song,
And with the flowers she comes again.

Yon bird is but her messenger,
The moon is but her silver car;
Yea! sun and moon are sent by her,
And every wistful waiting star.

— Richard LeGallienne

For Cremation Commitment Service

Fruit-Gathering: XL

O Fire, my brother, I sing victory to you.
  You are the bright red image of fearful freedom.
  You swing your arms in the sky, you sweep your impetuous
fingers across the harp-string, your dance music is beautiful.

  When my days are ended and the gates are opened you will
burn to ashes this cordage of hands and feet.
  My body will be one with you, my heart will be caught in
the whirls of your frenzy, and the burning heat that was my
life will flash up and mingle itself in your flame.

— Rabindranath Tagore

It is but fitting that we should commit this body
    to the flame
So like that which but recently did burn
Within that fine brave head.
It is as if he doth return
Unto the fountain whence he came,
Source of all spirits bright,
The comradeship and life of all pure souls,
As now he enters into purifying light.

— Robert Terry Weston

Additional Readings

"To W.P. II," by George Santayana
"Dirge Without Music," by Edna St. Vincent Millay
"Death," "Joy and Sorrow," and "Pain," from *The Prophet* by Kahlil
Gibran.
Psalms 19, 23 and 121.
  See also Death Ceremonies on pp. 67-80; and pp. 122-133.

REFERENCE

[1]Quotations by Robert Terry Weston, R.G. Ingersoll, Francis G. Ricker, Rev. John
G. MacKinnon, and Richard LeGallienne, are taken from *A Cup of Strength: Read-
ings in Time of Sorrow and Bereavement,* compiled by Robert Terry Weston, 1945.
Reprinted by permission from Robert Terry Weston.

Appendix IX / ANATOMICAL GIFTS

Information and Coordination

The American Association of Tissue Banks, 1117 N. 19th St., Suite 402, Arlington VA 22209 (703-528-0663). Non-governmental group of physicians, nurses, lawyers, technicians and the general public. Develops standards for tissue banking and encourages regional tissue banks.

The Living Bank, P.O. Box 6725, Houston TX 77265 (800-528-2971).

Medic Alert, Turlock CA 95380 (209-668-3333).

North American Transplant Coordinators Organization (*NATCO*), c/o Amy Peele, Rush-Presbyterian-St. Luke's Medical Center, 1753 West Congress Parkway, Chicago IL 60612 (800-24-DONOR). A professional organization of transplant coordinators; over 400 members.

Northern California Transplant Bank, P.O. Box 7999, San Francisco CA 94120 (415-922-3100—24-hour). Donations received from hospitals in No. Calif. and distributed nationally.

Organ Donors Canada, 5326 Ada Boulevard, Edmonton, Alberta T5W 4N7. Excellent source of information on anatomical gifts in Canada.

Uniform Donor Cards

Uniform Donor Cards may be obtained from *The Living Bank, Medic Alert* and *Organ Donors Canada* (addresses above); and from the *Continental Association of Funeral and Memorial Societies* (see Appendix VII) and *Kidney Foundations* (addresses on page 152.)

About Eye Banks

One important service we can render at death is to leave behind our eyes to relieve the blindness of others. In America alone there are about 30,000 blind people whose sight could be restored if enough corneas were available. Donated eyes may also be used for training and research. Not all vision defects can be cured by transplants and it is not possible to transfer the entire eye, but sight can be restored by corneal transplant in the great majority of cases of common corneal diseases.

To pledge your eyes, call or write the nearest Eye Bank. Also carry a Uniform Donor Card and be sure to check the Eye Bank square. Clear your plans with your family and let your physician know, in writing. No matter if you wear glasses, or what your age, race or blood type may be

Eyes must be removed within a few hours of death. This can be done in the hospital or at home, assuming trained personnel are available. Some funeral directors are trained to do this. Eyes may not be bequeathed to specific individuals, but must be used on a first-come first-serve basis regardless of ability to pay. Airlines fly them to their destinations without charge. Unlike other organs, the donation of eyes does not prevent leaving one's body to a medical school. Likewise, it makes no difference in the appearance of the body for viewing.

Canadian Eye Banks

ALBERTA: *Edmonton:* Eye Bank of Canada Alberta Division, c/o CNIB, 12010 Jasper Ave. T5K 0P3

BRITISH COLUMBIA: *Vancouver:* Eye Bank of Canada B.C. Division, c/o CNIB, 350 E. 36th Ave. V5W 1C6

MANITOBA: *Winnipeg:* Eye Bank of Canada Manitoba Division, c/o CNIB, 1031 Portage Ave. R3G 0R9

ONTARIO: *Toronto:* Eye Bank of Canada Ontario Division, 1929 Bayview Ave. M4G 3E8

QUEBEC: *Montreal:* La Banque D'Yeux du Quebec, Maisoneuve-Rosemont Hosp., 5689 Rosemont Blvd. H1T 2H1
    Ste Foy: La Banque D'Yeux De Laval

U.S. Eye Banks

ALABAMA: *Birmingham:* Alabama Lions Eye Bank, 708 W. 18th St. 35233 (205-871-3937)
    Tuskegee: Eye Bank of Central Alabama, 620 N. Water St. 36083 (205-727-6553)

ARIZONA: *Phoenix:* Arizona Lions Eye Bank, P.O. Box 13609 85002 (602-251-8100, ext. 295)

ARKANSAS: *Little Rock:* Arkansas Eye & Kidney Bank, 4301 W. Markham U.A.M.S. Slot 577 72205 (501-664-4990)

CALIFORNIA: *Fresno:* Lions Eye Bank of the San Joaquin Valley, Inc., P.O. Box 1232 93715 (209-442-EYES)
    Los Angeles: Lions Doheny Eye Bank, 1355 San Pablo Street 90033 (213 223-0333)
    Redondo Beach: So. Cal. Eye Bank & Research Foundation, 514 N. Prospect Ave. 90277 (213-376-9474, ext. 4602)
    Sacramento: Lions Eye & Tissue Bank, 4301 X St., Rm 251 95817 (916-453-2298)
    San Diego: San Diego Eye Bank, 4077 Fifth Ave. 92103-2180 (619-294-8267)

    San Francisco: Lions Eye Bank of No. Calif., P.O. Box 7999 94120 (415-922-3100)
    Santa Monica: Southern Calif. Lions Eye Institute, 1328 22nd St. 90404 (213-829-8579/829-8582)

COLORADO: *Denver:* Mountain States Eye Bank, 3500 E. 12th Ave. 80206 (303-399-6519)

CONNECTICUT: *New Britain:* Conn. Eye Bank, New Britain General Hospital 06052 (203-224-5550)

D.C.: *Washington:* Lions of District 22-C Eye Bank & Research Foundation, Inc., 1053 Buchanan St. NE 20017 (202-393-2265)

FLORIDA: *Gainesville:* North Fla. Lions Eye Gank, J. Hillis Miller Health Center, Box J-382 32610 (904-392-3135)
    Orlando: The Medical Eye Bank, Inc., 720 E. Colonial Dr. 32803 (305-422-2020)
    Tampa: Central Fla. Lions Eye Bank, 12901 N. 30th St., Box 21 33612 (813-977-1300)

GEORGIA: *Atlanta:* Ga. Lions Eye Bank, Inc., 1365 Clifton Rd NE 30322 (404-321-9300)
    Augusta: Ga. Lions Eye Bank-Augusta, Medical College of Ga. 30912 (404-724-1388)

HAWAII: *Honolulu:* Hawaii Lions Eye Bank & Makana Foundation, P.O. Box 2783 96803 (808-536-7416)

ILLINOIS: *Bloomington:* Mennonite Hospital-Watson Gailey Eye Foundation Eye Bank, 807 N. Main St. 61701 (309-827-4321/829-5311)

Chicago: Illinois Eye Bank, 53 W. Jackson Blvd., Rm 1435 60604 (312-922-8710)

INDIANA: *Indianapolis:* Indiana Lions Eye Bank, Inc., 702 Rotary Circle 46223 (317-264-8527/635-8431)

IOWA: *Iowa City:* Univ. Hospital, Dept of Opthalmology 52242 (319-356-2215/356-1616)

KANSAS: *Kansas City:* Kansas Odd Fellows Eye Bank, Inc., 39th & Rainbow 66103 (913-588-6658)

Wichita: Lions Eye Bank of Central Kansas, P.O. Box 1358 67201 (316-268-5144)

KENTUCKY: *Louisville:* Kentucky Lions Eye Foundation, 301 Muhammad Ali Blvd. 40202 (502-584-9934)

Lexington: Kentucky Lions Eye Bank-Univ. of Ky., 800 Rose St. 40356-0084 (606-233-5000, beeper #514)

LOUISIANA: *Baton Rouge:* Our Lady of the Lake Regional Medical Center, 5000 Hennessy Blvd. 70809 (504-769-3100)

New Orleans: Southern Eye Bank, 145 Elk Pl. 70112 (504-523-6343)

Shreveport: NW La. Lions Eye Bank, 2600 Greenwood Rd. 71103 (318-424-EYES)

MARYLAND: *Baltimore:* Medical Eye Bank, Inc., 505 Park Ave. 21201 (301-752-2020)

Bethesda: International Eye Bank, 7801 Norfolk Ave. 20814 (301-986-1830)

MASSACHUSETTS: *Boston:* New England Eye Bank, 243 Charles St. 02114 (617-523-7900)

MICHIGAN: *Ann Arbor:* Michigan Eye Bank, 1000 Wall St 48109 (313-764-3262)

Marquette: Upper Mich. Lions Eye Bank, Marquette Gen. Hosp., 420 W. Magentic St. 49855 (906-228-9440, ext. 580)

MINNESOTA: *Minneapolis:* Minn. Lions Eye Bank, Mayo Hospital, Box 493 55455 (612-373-4334/373-8312)

Rochester: Mayo Clinic Eye Bank, 200 SW First St. 55905 (507-284-3760)

MISSISSIPPI: *Jackson:* Miss. Lions Eye Bank, Inc., 2500 N. State St. 39216 (601-987-5899)

MISSOURI: *Columbia:* Mo. Lions Eye Tissue Bank, 404 Portland 65201 (314-443-1479)

Kansas City: Kansas City Eye Bank, Inc., 605 W. 47th St., Suite 228 64112 (816-531-1066)

St. Louis: Lions Eye Bank in St. Louis, 1325 S. Grand 63104 (314-771-7600)

St. Louis: St. Louis Eye Bank, 660 S. Euclid 63110 (314-454-2150/454-2666)

NEBRASKA: *Omaha:* Lions Eye Bank of Nebraska, 42nd & Dewey Ave. 68105 (402-559-4039)

NEVADA: *Las Vegas:* Nev. Eye Bank, 620 Shadow Lane 89106 (702-386-3937)

NEW JERSEY: *Newark:* N.J. Eye Bank, 15 S. 9th St. 07107 (201-456-4626)

NEW MEXICO: *Albuquerque:* N.M. Lions Eye Bank, 201 Cedar SE, Suite 601 87106 (505-841-1210)

NEW YORK: *Albany:* Sight Conservation Soc. of NE New York, Inc., 628 Madison Ave. 12208 (518-445-5199)

Buffalo: Buffalo Eye Bank & Research Society, Inc., 2550 Main St. 14214 (716-832-5448/835-8725)

New York: Eye Bank for Sight Restoration, 210 E 64th St. 10021 (212-980-6700/838-9211)

Rochester: Rochester Eye & Human Parts Bank, 220 Alexander St. 14607 (716-546-5250)

Syracuse: Central NY Eye Bank & Research Corporation, Upstate Medical Center, P.O. Box 21 13201 (315-471-6060)

NORTH CAROLINA: *Winston-Salem:* 3195 Maplewood Ave. 27103 (919-765-0932)

NORTH DAKOTA: *Williston:* The Williston Lions Eye Bank, Mercy Hospital, Box 1627 58801 (701-572-7661)

OHIO: *Cincinnati:* Cincinnati Eye Bank, 231 Bethesda Ave., Rm 6004 45267 (513-861-3716)

Cleveland: Cleveland Eye Bank, 1909 E. 101st St. 44106 (216-791-9700)

Columbus: Central Ohio Lions Eye Bank, Inc., 456 Clinic Dr., UHC 43210 (614-421-8114)

Youngstown: Melvin E. Jones Eye Bank, 2246 Glenwood Ave. 44511 (216-788-2411)

OKLAHOMA: *Oklahoma City:* Okla. Lions Eye Bank, Dean A. McGee Eye Inst. 608 S.L. Young Dr. 73104 (405-271-5691)

OREGON: *Portland:* Oregon Lions Eye Bank, 1200 NW 23rd St. 97210 (503-229-7523)

PENNSYLVANIA: *Erie:* Greater Erie Eye Bank, Inc., 2402 Cherry St. 16502-2693 (814-459-3534)

Hellertown: NE Pa. Lions Eye Bank, 100 Roth Ave. 18055 (215-252-3418)

Philadelphia: Lions Eye Bank of Delaware Valley, Wills Eye Hospital, 9th & Walnut Sts. 19107 (215-569-3937)

Pittsburgh: Medical Eye Bank of Western Pa. 3515 Fifth Ave. 15213 (412-687-8828)

PUERTO RICO: *Hato Rey:* P.R. Lions Eye Bank, Box 'O' 00919 (809-763-8050)

SOUTH CAROLINA: *West Columbia:* S.C. Lions Eye Bank, 110 Lexington Medical Mall 29169 (803-796-1304)

SOUTH DAKOTA: *Sioux Falls:* Lions Eye Bank of S.D., 800 W. Ave. N. 57104 (605-334-9383)

TENNESSEE: *Knoxville:* E. Tenn. Eye Bank, 509 Cedar Bluff Rd. N. 37923 (615-693-4991)

Memphis: Mid-South Eye Bank, P.O. Box 40627 38104 (901-726-8264)

Nashville: Lions Eye Bank and Sight Service, Medical Arts Bldg., Suite 634 37212 (615-322-2662)

TEXAS: *Abilene:* District 2-E1 Lions Eye Bank, Inc., 224 S. Leggett Dr. 79605 (915-673-7334)

Amarillo: Lions Hi-Plains Eye Bank of District 2-T1, Inc., 1600 Wallace Blvd. 79106 (806-359-5101)

Dallas: Lions Sight and Tissue Foundation, 5323 Harry Hines, Rm G7-250 75235 (214-688-3908)

El Paso: W. Texas Lions Eye Bank, 1801 N. Oregon St. 79902 (915-532-6281, ext. 1265/544-7750)

Fort Worth: Lions Organ & Eye Bank of District 2-E2, Inc., 1263 W. Rosedale 76104 (817-335-4935)

Houston: Lions Eyes of Texas Eye Bank, 6501 Fannin, Suite C-307 77030 (713-797-9270)

Lackland AFB: Central USAF Eye Bank, WHMC/SGHSE-Wilford Hall 78236 (512-670-7841)

Lubbock: District 2-T2 Lions Eye Bank, Bx 5901 79417 (806-762-2242)

Midland: District 2-A1 Lions Eye Bank, P.O. Box 4283 79704 (915-685-1550/697-1633)

San Antonio: Eye Bank at Baptist Memorial Hospital, 111 Dallas 78286 (512-222-8432, ext. 3510)

Temple: Lions Organ & Eye Bank of District 2-X3, Inc., 2401 S. 31 St., Rm W-177 76508 (817-773-0612)

Tyler: East Tex. Regional Eye Bank, P.O. Drawer 6400 75711 (214-597-0351)

UTAH: *Salt Lake City:* Lions Eye Bank of Univ. of Utah, 50 N. Medical Dr. 84132 (801-581-2039)

VIRGINIA: *Norfolk:* Lions Eye Bank & Research Center of Eastern Va., Inc., 600 Gresham Dr. 23507 (804-628-EYES)

Richmond: Old Dominion Eye Bank, 1001 E. Marshall St. 23219 (804-648-0890)

Roanoke: Eye Bank & Research Foundation of Virginia, Inc., P.O. Box 1772 24008 (703-345-8823)

WASHINGTON: *Seattle:* Lions Eye Bank of Wash. & No. Idaho, Dept of Opthalmology-RJ10 98195 (206-543-5394/543-3333)

WISCONSIN: *Madison:* Wisc Eye Bank-Madison, 600 Highland Ave. 53792 (608-263-6223)

Milwaukee: Wisc. Lions Bank, 8700 W. Wisconsin Ave. 53226 (414-257-5543)

The Bequeathal of Bodies to Schools of Medicine and Dentistry

Why They Are Needed: Bequeathals are increasing, but not fast enough. Also, greater sharing is needed between areas of surplus and shortage. Our 1983 survey showed a surplus of bodies in a few areas and shortages in others. Twenty-five schools reported "urgent" need, as compared with thirty-six schools in 1979 and 1976, thirty-four in 1974 and thirty in 1972.

Procedure at Time of Death: If there is to be no service in the presence of the body, as when a memorial service is held instead of a funeral service, then the body may be removed immediately to the medical school. In that case the directory of medical schools in this *Manual* should be consulted and a phone call made to the anatomy department of the nearest school listed as accepting bequeathals. Transportation details can be worked out on the phone. A funeral director usually takes the body to the school, though an ambulance is sometimes used, or the school may have its own conveyance. If no funeral director is used, someone else must handle the legal papers.

A Deeply Meaningful Experience: The papers are simple. The physician in charge signs a death certificate. This is taken to the county Board of Health where a transportation permit is issued. The body is then transported to the medical school where it is signed for. The family may prefer to take the body themselves, using a station wagon. This has been the practice in our family, and we would not think of turning it over to someone else. It is something we can do for the loved one and helps us to accept the loss. The legal formalities are simple, as explained above. The body may be placed in a box or on a stretcher or a plain canvas cot, or simply wrapped in a blanket. People are repelled by death and often shrink from handling a dead body. In practice, however, the privilege of helping to care for the body of a friend or a loved one is a deeply meaningful experience. Too often in modern life we withdraw from reality or call in a professional to do things we might benefit by doing for ourselves.

Transportation of the Remains: Some medical schools pay no transportation expenses. Most pay the expense within the state or within a certain radius (see the directory). Expenses beyond that distance are paid by the family. Incidentally, Amtrac offers fast, cheap service to some 300 points. In warm weather the body should be taken to the medical school within twenty-four hours, unless dry ice is used. The school will dispose of the remains, or, if desired, will return the ashes to the family.

If a common carrier is used, such as an airline or Amtrac, the body must be packed in a certain way, requiring the services of a funeral director. If the body is to be held for a funeral service or sent by common carrier, the funeral director should ask the medical school what kind of embalming is acceptable to the school. If the body is delivered promptly, in a private vehicle, no embalming is necessary.

Alternative Plans: It is important to have an alternative plan, preferably through a memorial society. We are pleased to report that for the first time since we started publishing this *Manual* twenty-two years ago, bequeathals are gaining on the needs. While most schools continue to have urgent or moderate need, an increasing number are amply supplied and may or may not accept bequeathals at any given time. Furthermore, a body which is mutilated or autopsied or is otherwise in bad condition, or from which organs other than eyes have been removed, is not acceptable. Likewise, some diseases disqualify a body for medical school use.

Medical Schools of Canada and the U.S.

This information was compiled with the help of the schools of medicine, dentistry and osteopathy in the United States, Canada and Puerto Rico. It includes the degree of need of each school for the bequeathal of bodies and the distance, if any, from which the school will pay transportation. This list is in geo-alphabetical sequence.

Key	Degree of Need:	Transportation Paid:
	U- Urgent Need	*W/S*-Within state
	M-Moderate Need	*W/P*-Within province
	A - Supplies ample	*150 mi*-Within that radius
	N- No bequeathals accepted	*Local*-Local area only
		None-No transportation paid

Directory

Canadian Medical Schools

M- U. of Calgary, Faculty of Medicine, 3350 Hospital Dr. NW, Calgary ALTA T2N 4N1 (403-284-6950)—[*$125*]

U- U. of Alberta, Faculty of Medicine, Edmonton, ALTA (432-3355)—[*150 mi*]

M- U. of B.C., Faculty of Medicine, Vancouver, BC (228-2498)—[*Local*]

M- U. of Manitoba, Faculty of Medicine, Winnipeg, MAN R3E 0W3 (786-3652)—[*$50*]

U- Memorial U., Faculty of Medicine, St. Johns, NFLD A1B 3V6 (737-6727)—[*W/P*]

Dalhousie U., Faculty of Medicine, Tupper Medical Bldg., Halifax, N.S.

M- McMaster U., Dept. of Anatomy, 1200 Main St., Hamilton, ONT L8N 3Z5 (525-9140)—[*Local*]

A- Queen's U., Faculty of Medicine, Dept. of Anatomy, Kingston, ONT K7L 3N6 (547-2600)—[*W/P, $120*]

M- U. of Western Ontario, Med. School, Dept. of Anatomy, London, ONT (679-3741)—[*None*]

M- U. of Ottawa, Anatomy Dept., Health Sciences Center, 451 Smyth Rd, Ottawa, ONT K1H 8M5 (737-6613/6504) —[*None*]

M- U. of Toronto, Anatomy Dept., Fac. of Medicine, Toronto, ONT M5S 1A8 (978-2011/2692)—[*None*]

M- McGill U., Dept. of Anatomy, 3640 Univ. St., Montreal, P.Q. H3A 2B2 (392-4535)—[*Local*]

M- U. de Montreal, Faculte de Med., 2900 Blvd. Edward Montpetit, Montreal, P.Q. H3C 3J7 (343-6290)—[*100 mi*]

A- Dept. d'Anatomie, Universite Laval, Quebec, P.Q. G1K 7P4 (656-3090/681-6611)—[*100 mi*]

N- U. of Sherbrooke, Faculty of Medicine, Sherbrooke, P.Q. (563-5555/565-2081)—*150 mi*]

M- U. of Saskatchewan, Col. of Med., Dept. of Anatomy, Saskatoon, SASK (343-2661)—[*W/P*]

U.S. Medical Schools

M- U. of Alabama, Anatomy Dept., University Station, Birmingham AL 35294 (934-4494)—[*W/S*]

M- U. of South Alabama, Dept. of Anatomy, Mobile AL 36608 (460-6490)—[*None*]

A- U. of Arizona, College of Medicine, Anatomy Dept., Tucson AZ 85724 (626-6084)—[*W/S*]

A- U. of Arkansas, College of Medicine, Anatomy Dept., Little Rock AR 72205 (661-5180)—[*W/S*]

M- U. of Calif. at Davis, School of Med., Dept. of Human Anatomy, Davis CA 95616 (752-2100)—[*30 mi*]

M- U. of Calif. at Irvine, Anatomy Dept., College of Med., Irvine CA 92717 (856-6061)—[*50 mi*]

M- U. of Calif. at San Diego, Sch. of Med., Learning Resources Office, La Jolla CA 92093 (452-4536)—[*County*]

M- Loma Linda U. School of Med., Anatomy Dept., Loma Linda CA 92354 (824-4301)—[*None*]

M- U. of Calif. at L.A., Anatomy Dept., School of Med., Los Angeles CA 90024 (825-9563)—[*50 mi*]

A- U. of So. Calif. School of Medicine, 1333 San Pablo St., L.A. CA 90033 (222-0231/228-7825)—[*50 mi*]

U- Col. of Osteopathic Med. of the Pacific, 309 Pomona Mall E., Pomona CA 91766 (623-6116)—[*50 mi*]

M- Calif. State Polytechnic Univ., Pomona CA 91768 (598-4459/4444)—[*50 mi*]

U- U. of Calif. at S.F., School of Medicine, Anatomy Dept., San Francisco CA 94143 (666-1981/9000)—[*None*]

M- Anatomy Dept., School of Medicine, Stanford U., Stanford CA 94305 (497-2404)—[*10 mi*]

M- U. of Colorado, School of Medicine, 4200 E. 9th Ave., Denver CO 80262 (394-8554/399-1211)—[*Local*]

M- U. of Conn. School of Medicine, Farmington Ave., Farmington CT 06032 (223-4340)—[*W/S*]

U- Yale U. School of Medicine, New Haven CT 06510 (436-4219/785-2813)—[*W/S*]

M- Georgetown U. School of Medicine, Anatomy Dept., Washington DC 20007 (625-2271)—[*25 mi*]

A- Howard U. College of Dentristry, 600 W St. NW, Washington DC 20001 (636-6400)

M- Howard U. College of Med., Washington DC 20059 (636-6555)—[*Local*]

U- Geo. Washington U. Anatomy Dept., 2300 I St. NW, Washington DC 20037 (676-3511)—[*50 mi*]

M- Anatomical Board of Fla, U. of Fla., Coll. of Med., Gainesville FL 32610 (392-3588/372-0837)—[*None*]

A- U. of Miami School of Med., Anatomy Dept., Miami FL 33101 (547-6691/284-2211)

A- Anatomy Dept., Coll. of Med., U. of South Florida, 12901 N 30th St., Tampa FL 33612 (974-2843)—[*None*]

M- Emory U. School of Med., Anatomy Dept., Atlanta GA 30322 (329-6242)—[*50 mi*]

U- Dept. of Anatomy, Morehouse School of Med., 720 Westview Dr. SW, Atlanta GA 30310 (752-1014/971-8663)—[*500 mi*]

M- Med. College of Ga., School of Med., Anatomy Dept., Augusta GA 30912 (404-828-3731)—[*W/S*]

M- Mercer U. School of Med., 1550 College St., Macon GA 31207 (744-2600/2700)—[*Local*]

A- U. of Hawaii, Dept. of Anatomy & Repro. Biol., Hawaii State Anatomical Bd., 1960 East-West Rd., Honolulu HI 96822 (948-7131)—[*Local*]

U- Demonstrators Assoc. of Ill., 2240 W. Filmore, Chicago IL 60612 (733-5283)—[*None*]

M- Ind. State Anatomical Bd., Ind. U., Med. Center, Indianapolis IN 46223 (264-7494/786-4256)—[*None*]

U- College of Osteopathic Med. & Surgery, Health Sciences, 3200 Grand Ave., Des Moines IA 50312 (515-271-1400)

A- U. of Iowa, Coll. of Med., Dept of Anatomy, Iowa City IA 52242 (356-1616/353-5905)—[*None*]

M- U. of Kansas Med. Center, 39th & Rainbow Blvd., Kansas City KS 66103 (913-588-7000)—[*Local*]

M- U. of Kentucky Coll. of Med., Lexington KY 40536-0084 (233-5276/5811) —[*W/S*]

M- U. of Louisville Sch. of Med., Health Sciences Center, Louisville KY 40292 (588-5165)—[*50 mi*]

Univ. of New England, Coll. of Osteopathic Med., 605 Pool Rd., Biddeford ME 04005 (283-0171)—[*W/S*]

M- Bureau of Anatomical Svcs., Dept. of Anatomy, Tulane U. Sch. of Med., 1430 Tulane Ave., New Orleans LA 70112 (588-5255)—[*W/S*]

M- State Anatomy Board, 655 W. Baltimore, Rm B-026, Baltimore MD 21201 (547-1222)—[*W/S*]

U- Uniformed Services Univ. of the Health Sciences, 4301 Jones Bridge Rd., Bethesda MD 20814 (295-3333)—[*150 mi*]

M- Coordinator of Anatomical Gifts, 55 Lake Ave N., Worcester MA 01605 (856-2458)—[*W/S*]

M- U. of Mich. Med. Sch., 3736 Med. Science II, Ann Arbor MI 48109 (764-4359)—[*150 mi*]

M- Wayne State U. Sch. of Med., 540 E. Canfield, Detroit MI 48201 (577-1188/ 1198)—[*Local*]

A- Mich. State U., Anatomy Dept., E. Lansing MI 48823 (355-1855)—[*Local*]

A- U. of Minn. Coll. of Med. Science, Anatomy Bequest Program, 2-155 Jackson Hall, 321 Church St., University of Minnesota, Minneapolis MN 55455 (373-2776)—[*Local*]

U- U. of Miss. Medical Center, Jackson MS 39216 (987-4561)—[*Local*]

In Missouri make bequeathals to individual schools, or to:

M- Missouri State Anatomical Bd., U. of Missouri, Columbia MO 65212 (882-2288)—[*None*]

A- Anatomical Bd. of Nebraska, 42nd & Dewey Aves., Omaha NE 68105 (559-6249)—[*W/S*]

M- U. of Nev., Sch. of Med., Reno NV 89557 (784-6113)—[*None*]

M- Dartmouth Med. Sch., Anatomy Dept., Hanover NH 03755 (646-7636/ 7640)—[*W/S*]

M- Fairleigh Dickinson U., Sch. of Dentristy, 110 Fuller Pl., Hackensack NJ 07601 (863-6300/748-0240)—[*100 mi*]

M- U. of Med. and Dentistry of NJ, 100 Bergen St., Newark NJ 07103 (201-456-4648)—[*W/S*]

A- CMDNJ-Rutgers Med. Sch., PO Box 101, Piscataway NJ 08854 (564-4580)— [*W/S*]

A- U. of N.M., Anatomy Dept., No. Campus, Albuquerque NM 87131 (277-2555)—[*Local*]

M- Anatomical Gift Prog., Dept of Anatomy, Albany Med. Coll., 47 New Scotland Ave., Albany NY 12208 (445-5379) —[*150 mi*]

U- Downstate Med. Center, 450 Clarkson Ave., Brooklyn NY 11203 (270-1027/ 1053)—[*100 mi*]

A- State U. of NY at Buffalo, Sch. of Med., Anatomy Dept., Buffalo NY 14214 (831-2912)—[*100 mi*]

U- Anatomical Gift Registry, PO Box 1664, New York NY 10001 (596-4444)

U- Columbia U. Coll. of Physicians & Surgeons, 630 W 168th St., New York, NY 10032 (694-3451)—[*100 mi*]

U- Cornell U. Med. Coll. 1300 York Ave. New York NY 10021 (472-6400)—[*None*]

M- Mt. Sinai Med. Ctr., One Gustave L. Levy Pl., New York NY 10029 (650-7057) —[*150 mi*]

M- N.Y. Univ. Sch. of Med., 550 First Ave., New York NY 10016 (340-5378)— [*Local*]

U- Yeshiva U., Albert Einstein Col. of Med., Eastchester Rd. & Morris Park Ave., New York NY 10461 (430-2837)— [*50 mi*]

A- U. of Rochester Sch. of Med., 601 Elmwood Ave., Rochester NY 14642 (275-2591/2272)—[*Local*]

M- Anatomical Sciences, Health Sci. Ctr., Stony Brook NY 11794 (444-2350)— [*50 mi*]

U- State U. of NY, Upstate Med. Ctr., Anatomy Dept., 766 Irving Ave., Syracuse NY 13210 (473-5120)—[*W/S*]

U- N.Y. Med. Coll., Basic Science Bldg, Valhalla NY 10595 (347-5630/5620)—[*50 mi*]

M- U. of N.C. School of Medicine, Chapel Hill NC 27514 (966-1237/286-2576)—[*330 mi*]

M- Duke Med. Center, Anatomy Dept., Durham NC 27710 (684-4124)—[*100 mi*]

A- E. Carolina U., Sch. of Med., Greenville NC 27834 (757-2849)—[*W/S*]

A- Bowman Gray Sch. of Med., Winston-Salem NC 27103 (723-5813/748-4368)—[*W/S or 200 mi*]

M- U. of North Dakota Sch. of Med., Grand Forks ND 58201 (777-2101)—[*W/S*]

U- Ohio U. Coll. of Osteopathic Med., Athens OH 45701 (594-6401)—[*W/S*]

M- U. of Cincinnati Coll. of Med., Cincinnati OH 45267 (872-5611/5674)—[*None*]

M- Case Western Reserve Sch. of Med., 2119 Abington Rd., Cleveland OH 44106 (368-3430/221-9330)—[*75 mi*]

M- Ohio State U., Anatomy Dept., 333 W 10th Ave., Columbus OH 43210 (422-4831)—[*W/S*]

A- Wright State U., Sch. of Med., Dr. Frank Nagy, Director, Donated Body Program, Dept., of Anatomy, Dayton OH 45435 (873-3066)—[*W/S*]

Northeastern Ohio Universities Coll. of Med., Rootstown OH 44272 (325-2511 ext. 255)

M- Med. Coll. of Ohio at Toledo, C.S. 10008, 3000 Arlington Ave., Toledo OH 43699 (381-4109)—[*None*]

U- U. of Okla. Health Sciences Center, Box 26901, Oklahoma City OK 73190 (271-2424)—[*W/S*]

M- Okla. Coll. of Osteopathic Med. & Surgery, Tulsa OK 74101 (582-1972)—[*W/S*]

U. of Okla., Tulsa Medical College, Tulsa OK 74105 (749-5530)

M- Oregon Health Sciences Univ., Sch. of Med., Anatomy Dept., Portland OR 97201 (225-8302/7888)—[*None*]

U- Humanity Gifts Registry of Pa., 130 S 9th St., #1455, Philadelphia PA 19107 (922-4440)—[*W/S, $50*]

M- Brown U., Div. of Biology & Med., Providence RI 02912—[*W/S*]

M- Medical University of S.C., 171 Ashley Ave., Charleston, SC 29425 (792-3521)—[*W/S*]

M- Univ. of S. Dakota, Sch. of Med., Vermillion SD 57069 (624-3923/677-5321)—[*300 mi*]

A- E. Tenn. State U. Coll. of Med., Anatomy Dept., Box 19960-A, Johnson City TN 38614 (928-6426)—[*150 mi*]

M- U. of Tenn. Center for Health Sci., 875 Monroe Ave., Memphis TN 38163 (528-5965/5500)—[*W/S*]

U- Meharry Med. College, 1005 18th Ave. N., Nashville TN 37208 (327-6308/244-0375)—[*300 mi*]

A- Vanderbilt U. Sch. of Med., Anatomy Dept., Nashville TN 37232 (322-2134)—[*50 mi*]

M- Texas A&M U., Anatomy Dept., Medical Coll., College Station TX 77843 (845-4913/822-1571)—[*W/S*]

M- Baylor Dental School, 3302 Gaston, Dallas TX 76226 (824-6321 ext. 8270/828-8270)—[*W/S*]

M- U. of Tex., Health Science Ctr., 5323 Harry Hines, Dallas TX 75235 (688-2221)—[*50 mi*]

U- Tex. Coll. of Osteopathic Med., Anatomy Dept., Camp Bowie Blvd. at Montgomery, Ft. Worth TX 76107 (735-2000)—[*Local*]

M- U. of Tex., Medical Branch, Galveston TX 77550 (409-761-1293/763-0200)—[*300 mi*]

A- Baylor Coll. of Med., 1200 Moursund Houston TX 77025 (713-799-4930)—[*W/S, 250 mi*]

A- U. of Tex. Health Sci. Ctr. at Houston P.O. Box 20708, Houston TX 77025 (792-5703)—[*W/S*]

A- Tex. Tech U., Sch of Med., Anatomy Dept., Lubbock TX 79430 (743-2700/3111)—[*360 mi*]

U- Tex. Chiropractic Coll., 5912 Spencer Hwy., Pasadena TX 77505 (487-1170—[*100 mi*]

A- U. of Tex. Health Sci. Ctr., 7703 Floyd Curl Dr., San Antonio TX 78284 (512-691-6533)—[*100 mi*]

M- U. of Utah, Sch. of Med., Dept. of Anatomy, Salt Lake City UT 84132 (581-6728/582-3711)—*[50 mi]*

U- U. of Utah Physical Therapy Prog., Bldg. 206, Salt Lake City UT 84112 (581-8681)—*[150 mi]*

M- U. of Vt., Coll. of Med., Dept. of Anatomy, Burlington VT 05405 (656-2230/3131)—*[None]*

A- E. Va. Med. School, Dept. of Anatomy, Box 1980, Norfolk VA 23501 (446-5640/786-2479)—*[W/S]*

A- State Anatomical Div., Dept of Health, Richmond VA 23219 (786-2479)—*[W/S]*

M- U. of Wash., Dept. of Biological Structure, SM-20, Sch. of Med., Seattle WA 98195 (543-1860)—*[Local]*

M- Marshall U. School of Med., Huntington WV 25701 (429-6788)—*[W/S]*

M- W. Va. Sch. of Osteopathic Med., Human Gift Registry. 400 N. Lee St., Lewisburg WV 24901 (645-6270)—*[W/S]*

M- W. Va. U., Med. Ctr., Human Gift Registry, Morgantown WV 26506 (293-6322)—*[W/S]*

M- U. of Wisc. Med. School, 325 SMI, Madison WI 53706 (262-2888)—*[W/S]*

A- The Med. Coll. of Wisc., Dept. of Anatomy, 8701 Watertown Plank Rd., Milwaukee WI 53226 (414-257-8261/8262)—*[Local]*

U- Anatomy Board of Puerto Rico, Ofc. 503, 5th Fl., Med. Sci. Bldg., San Juan PR 00936 (753-5223)—*[W/S]*

Specific Anatomical Gifts (see also Eye Banks and Medical Schools)

Ear Drums and Ear Bones: Persons with *normal* hearing can bequeath parts to restore the hearing to others. Project HEAR alone has provided 10,000 units of ear tissue for fourteen different types of implants since 1969. Medical information provided in advance is helpful. For further information contact Project HEAR, 1801 Page Mill Road, Palo Alto CA 94304, or The Ear Bank of British Columbia, 865 West 10th Ave., Vancouver, B.D. V5Z 1L7. Persons with hearing problems or other *ear disorders* are urged to bequeath ear structures for research. A medical history is obtained from the donor's doctor. Removal of ear structures is a specialized task. Arrangements are made in the U.S. by the National Temporal Bone Banks Center of the Deafness Research Foundation, 55 East 34th St., New York NY 10016, and in Canada by the Ontario Temporal Bone Bank of the Banting Institute, University of Toronto, Toronto Ontario M5G 1L5.

Kidneys: First and most frequent of major organs to be transplanted, about 23,000 kidneys were transplanted in the U.S. from 1978 to 1983. In Canada, twenty-two centers now transplant kidneys. The survival rate after one year is now as high as 97% for kidneys from related donors and 90% with cadaver organs.[1] In 1983, 65,000 people were kept alive by artificial kidney machines; 10,000 of these were waiting for a kidney transplant but only 5,358 received one because of a shortage of suitable donors.[2] For further information contact the National Kidney Foundation, 2 Park Ave., New York NY 10016, or the Kidney Foundation of Canada, Suite 400, 1650 de Maisonneuve Blvd. West, Montreal Quebec H3H 2P3. Consult telephone directory or national office for addresses of local and state or provincial offices.

Livers: A fairly recent development. *Newsweek* reported in 1983 that 540 transplants had been done.[3] One-year survival rates since the introduction of cyclosporin have doubled and now range up to 70%.[4]

Hearts: A total of 500 transplants were reported as of August, 1983, with 78% of patients surviving more than one year.

Pancreas: Primarily for diabetic patients, 334 transplants were reported as of August 1983 with a 25% success rate. The remaining 75% of patients were sustained on insulin medication.

Lungs: Thirty-eight lung transplants and twenty-two combined heart-lung transplants were reported as of August, 1983, with thirteen recipients of the combined organs still surviving.[5]

Pituitary Glands: An estimated 3,000 to 4,000 children in the U.S. require hormones extracted from pituitary glands to maintain normal growth. It takes the hormone of from 30 to 40 pituitaries per year to maintain normal growth for one child. A synthetic hormone is in the offing, but is likely to be expensive. More pituitaries are urgently needed as they are the source of other badly needed hormones that cannot be synthesized. Donor cards and further information may be had from National Hormone and Pituitary Program, Suite 501-9, 210 W. Fayette St., Baltimore, MD 21201-3472, or MRC Human Pituitary Hormone Committee, Department of Physiology, University of Manitoba, 770 Bannatyne Ave., Winnipeg Manitoba R3E 0W3.

Skin: Skin is valuable both for grafting and as dressing for burns. Dr. David Herndon of Shriners Burn Institute of Galveston says, ''The donation and application of human skin is the most significant advance in treating burns in the last twenty years, in terms of reducing patient mortality.''

Blood: This is the most commonly ''transplanted'' tissue, some ten million units (pints) being transfused annually in the U.S. alone. There has been some experimentation with the use of cadaver blood, which has some advantages, but this is not as yet being practiced because of prohibitive costs.

There is still a great need for volunteer donation of blood. The shortage of volunteer blood has led to the widespread use of commercial blood, with a resultant high rate of post-transfusion hepatitis. Transmission of the Acquired Immune Deficiency Syndrome (AIDS) is another risk increased by use of paid donors. While blood may be tested for hepatitis, there is not now a test for AIDS. Volunteers have no reason to conceal their health records; paid donors do. For further information contact the Blood Services Laboratories, American Red Cross, 9312 Old Georgetown Road, Bethesda MD 20814, or Canadian Red Cross Blood Transfusion Service, 95 Wellesley Street E., Toronto Ontario M4Y 1H6.

Brain Tissue: Post mortem research into Alzheimer's disease, Parkinson's disease, epilepsy, multiple sclerosis and other disorders involving brain pathology is being conducted with donated brain and other nerve tissues. Normal brain tissue is also ''urgently needed'' for this research. Contact the Canadian Brain Tissue Bank, Room 128, Banting Institute, 100 College Street, Toronto Ontario M5G 1L5; or the National Alzheimer's Disease

Brain Bank, c/o Dr. G. Glenner, University of California at San Diego School of Medicine (M-012), La Jolla CA 92093 (619-452-9616), for autopsy protocol.

Other Tissues: Many other tissues are valuable in promting health and saving lives—among them cartilage, iliac crests, dura mater, fascia lata, joints and bone marrow.

Artificial Implants: With the increasing use of artificial implants, including limbs, pacemakers, bone wire and screws, joints and others, there is a great need for research on how such implants perform and interact with human tissue once in place. Post mortem donation of such devices, with permission to analyze related tissues, can be extremely helpful in hospitals where such research is done.

REFERENCES

[1] Joan Arehart-Treichel, "The Organ Transplant Odyssey," *Science News*, October 1, 1983, 124:14, p.218.

[2] Fact sheet from National Kidney Foundation.

[3] *Newsweek*, "The New Era of Transplants," Aug. 19, 1983, pp. 38-44.

[4] Joan Arehart-Treichel, *op. cit.*

[5] *Newsweek*, *op. cit.*, is source for statistics on heart, pancreas and lung transplants.

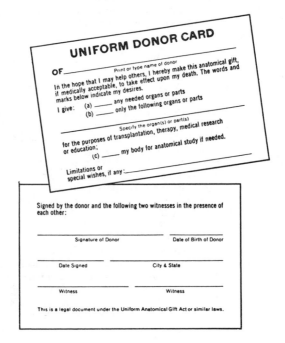

INDEX